If this is the Microwave, why am I getting Cable TV?

THE HANDYPERSON'S GUIDE TO THE KITCHEN

TIM THOMPSON, P. Eng

Deidre

To my intrepid friend;
This cooking stuff is
not so bad but just
in case this book
should help.

To a New beginning

Love
Kay

Published by
Creative Bound Inc.
P.O. Box 424, Carp, Ontario
Canada K0A 1L0

ISBN 0-921165-23-4
Printed and bound in Canada

Book design and Art Direction by Wendelina O'Keefe
Illustrations: (cover, pages 8 & 155) Mary Moore inspired by original drawing by Lynda Pitre
Computer Illustrations: Tim Thompson

Canadian Cataloguing in Publication Data

Thompson, Tim, date
    If this is the microwave, why am I getting cable T.V. ?

Includes index.
ISBN 0-921165-23-4

    1. Cookery.   2. Quick and easy cookery.   I. Title.

TX652.T46   1992   641.5   C92-090642-7

TABLE OF CONTENTS

PREFACE   7

LIST OF ACRONYMS   9

INTRODUCTION
    I would cook if I could only find the kitchen   11

1. THE KITCHEN WORKSHOP
    What's in the tool crib   15

2. PLANNING
    They even have MRP here   21

3. FOOD PREPARATION
    No Problem! (If you can open the package)   29

4. PROTOTYPES
    Nobody minds if you make mistakes   39

5. DEVELOPMENT MODELS
    Time to start getting serious   55

6. MATURE PRODUCTS
    Start thinking about GMP   65

7. FIELD SUPPORT
    Where all the dirty work is done   109

8. SOFTWARE
    Very User Friendly   131

9. THE FAT (FAMILY ACCEPTANCE TEST)
    How to Manage Turkeys   147

APPENDECTOMY
    Removing the Myth From Metric   157

DEDICATION

This book is dedicated to all scientists, engineers, students, statisticians and other persons who have passed from cooking the results to passing around the results of their cooking.

Acknowledgements

*I*t is very important for an author to acknowledge in writing the assistance given to him by other people when writing a book. This allows him to pass on some of the blame if he has to. Accordingly I would like to thank the following people. Jim and Donny Macmillan who encouraged me to continue after I had written the first chapter, and who subsequently read every word of the first manuscript, and offered many suggestions. Gail Pike and Wendy O'Keefe from Creative Bound Inc. for their unbounded enthusiasm and help. Dorothy Chan for saving me many hours of work by showing me how to do a concordance file in WordPerfect, and Bob Fenske who convinced me that it really was a "career change opportunity." The list would not be complete without thanking members of my family who were very positive in their support, so thanks to Michelle and Jeff for their help and many suggestions and to Jeff for suggesting the title. Also Lynda for creating the original handyman picture and last, but not least, my wife Pam, who insisted that I perfect each recipe before including it in this book, and who ate the results with a smile on her face (or was it a grimace?).

PREFACE

*I*n this day and age many people are suddenly thrust into a situation where they have to cope with unexpected meal preparation. This particulary applies to, but is not limited to, men who find themselves at home with a working wife. Sometimes the wife is away on a business trip, sometimes they arrive home from work before her, and sometimes they no longer have work to go to. These men then fit into the category of househusband, perhaps full time, perhaps part time. They are faced with the problem of preparing something edible, and although they are quite capable of reading a workshop manual, they have difficulty following recipes because the expressions are unfamiliar and the word barbecue doesn't appear once.

This book bridges the gap which exists between the complete neophyte, whether they be man or woman, who doesn't even know where the kitchen is, and the experienced kitchen technologist who can whip up a full course meal while bathing the baby. It is intended for all people who believe that they would be able to cook quite easily if only there was a handbook to follow. The book does not give instructions on bathing the baby.

At Home
All Alone
Twelve Noon
Eat Soon
Eggs Break
Toast Make
Meal Ready
Hold Steady
Toast Black
Eggs Slack
Meal Bad
Very Sad
Learn to Cook
Open Book

LIST OF ACRONYMS

In the modern world the acronym rules supreme. The following acronyms have been used in this book to ensure that readers do not suffer from AWS.

AWS	Acronym Withdrawal Syndrome
BOM	Bill Of Materials
CANS	Cook A Nice Supper
CANSD	Cook A Nice Supper Dear
FAT	Family Acceptance Test
FDA	Family Dining Area
GM	Grandmother
GMP	Good Meal Preparation
HICK	Househusband In Charge of the Kitchen
HOH	Head of Household
MRP	Meal Recipe Planning
SAR	Sauces and Relishes
TD	Turkey Dinner
WTH	Wow! That's Hot

INTRODUCTION
I would cook if I could only find the kitchen

It could never happen to you, but it has! You are now a househusband! Perhaps your wife has run off with your best friend, or did she run off with *her* best friend (lets face it in this day and age anything is possible). Has your spouse been promoted to Company President and decided that your place is in the home, or has she been promoted to sergeant and requested a transfer to another base?

Maybe you have followed a different scenario to become a househusband. You were a regular hard working guy when the company president (not your wife) called everybody together with the good news that it was payday and the bad news that the company was bankrupt and there was no pay. Or did that turkey who was your boss call you into his office and muttering words like Economy, Downsizing and Career Change Opportunity, ask you to clean off your workbench or desk and depart forthwith?

Regardless of how you got there you are now a househusband. Your wife has gone off to work after muttering sweet nothings in your ear like "Cook a nice supper tonight dear" and with a smirk on her face has roared off down the road with the family car. Although its nice to use your time at home to dream about ways of getting back at that turkey at work, forget about it and think positively; remember, in the kitchen it is quite legitimate to roast turkeys, and by the end of the book you will know how.

This book takes you step by step through the mysteries of the kitchen, and describes cooking in terms which you will understand. It assumes that you have a little background knowledge of the business and manufacturing industry including contact with government specifications, and that you have been involved in some home improvement projects. The chapters are arranged in sequence to introduce you to the technology of simple cooking, and to move you up gradually to more complex recipes so that you acquire the ability to 'Cook A Nice Supper' which has been abbreviated to CANS. Chapter headings are in words you are probably familiar with: Prototypes where you can experiment and try new cooking techniques, Development Models where you can put these ideas into practice and put together simple recipes, and finally the realization of the Mature Product where you prepare complete meals. Of course you need some Field Support (vegetables), and don't overlook the Software (dessert). Vital production aids such as MRP (Meal Recipe Planning) have been included. Finally you must pass the FAT (Family Acceptance Test).

FINDING THE KITCHEN

The first thing you must do is find the kitchen. A good place to start looking is in the vicinity of the beer fridge. If you have to open a door and go down more than five steps to the beer fridge then it is probably not in the kitchen, so look for another fridge. Eventually you should find a room which contains a refrigerator and also a square or rectangular box with little dials and some black circular or square gizmos on the top. The box should have a door at the front which pulls down to open. You have now found the stove, which is what this book is all about. If the box doesn't have the gizmos on top, but still has a door which opens down, then you have located the drier which is not what this book is about. You are probably in the laundry room or the local laundromat; return to GO and start again. Don't give up until you find the kitchen and the stove.

When you are sure you are in the kitchen, look around. The minimum you should find is a stove, a fridge (with or without beer), a workbench and a sink with taps. There should also be some cupboards above and below the workbench. These are usually set so that they are too high for someone to reach the top shelf, or if you can reach the top shelf they are designed so that you cannot see into the bottom shelf of the lower cupboards. This is an example of traditional kitchen design. There is also nowhere to sit while working, that is also traditional. Now you know why your wife goes out to work.

INTRODUCTION TO THE KITCHEN

Now that you have found the kitchen let's take stock, starting first with terminology. The work benches are called counter tops or kitchen tables and are usually covered with some form of plastic sheeting which is "easy" to clean. This is true providing you clean up spills immediately; if you leave them to dry you will find that spills stick better than any glue. Warning: Don't use the power sander to clean them off or you'll scratch the surface and the spill will stick even better next time; clean them up immediately with a soft wet cloth.

> **Tip**: If food does accidently dry on the counter top and is difficult to remove, place a damp cloth over it for 10 to 15 minutes and it will wipe clean easily.

On top of the counter top you will probably find many things: the dirty breakfast dishes (make sure that you do these before the boss gets home), a pot of luke warm coffee or tea, some jars or tins labelled 'tea', 'coffee', etc. which are probably filled with anything but 'tea', 'coffee', etc., and some strange looking electric tools with cords attached which are much cleaner than the ones you used at work. Kitchen tools with cords attached are called appliances and these fall into three categories: small, large, and broken. The classification is simple: if they will fit on the counter top or in a cupboard they are small, if they are too big to do this they are large and if they are on your work bench in the basement they are broken and I can guarantee that you still won't have time to fix them.

There are many small appliances designed for kitchen use, some are more useful than others and they fit into two basic groups: those designed to help in food preparation (mixers, shredders, slicers, etc.), and those which can be used for heating food (microwave ovens, toasters, slow cookers, etc.).

Major appliances consist of the fridge and stove and possibly a dishwasher. Some households even have several dishwashers aged between six and sixteen who approach the task with the same enthusiasm that they do their homework.

Locate all the small appliances and determine which group they fit into. If they whir when they are switched on they are for preparing food, if they get warm they are for cooking, and if they smell of burnt insulation or do nothing they are broken.

> **Tip**: Don't use the iron as a small cooking appliance unless you want fried egg on your shirt collars.

A word of caution, some heating appliances have small cooling fans inside which also whir, but softly. Don't try using these fans for food preparation; remember what happens if you are too close when something hits the fan.

An introduction to the kitchen would not be complete without a look in the cupboards and drawers. Check the contents of each cupboard carefully, you might find that screwdriver you lost last year in the process. Some cupboards will have packets or tins of food on the shelves; you can recognize these because the packets and tins will have coloured photographs of culinary delights on the outside. Don't be misled. When the can is opened, the contents will barely resemble the pictures. Be careful in your identification. If it has anything resembling a cat or a dog in the picture then it's pet food, no matter how appetizing it might look.

These cupboards contain your main product inventory, so make a note of everything you have. Your list may look something like this:

    1 can tomato soup
    1 can (no label)
    23 cans evaporated milk
    1/2 packet of something you've never heard of
    1/4 packet rice
    1 free sample package 'One cup coffee filters'
    6 packets of enchilada mix
    etc.

This list will show you what you do not need to buy next time you go to the grocery store. Don't forget to include the pet food in your inventory, particularly if you have a pet. If you don't have a pet you should definitely keep a record just in case you realize one can is missing just after you've opened a can of beef stew.

Other cupboards or shelves will have dishes and bowls. The bowls will be useful for mixing later on, so note which cupboard they are in. Finally, check out all the kitchen drawers. Some will contain normal eating utensils, others may contain much larger spoons and forks, together with some large sharp knives. Again remember where everything is, so that you can find it later on. One drawer will probably contain junk. This is the 'C' drawer of the kitchen where everything goes which has no obvious application, but which cannot be thrown out. Beware of kitchens in which every drawer is a C drawer — you'll never find anything.

That completes the introduction to the basic kitchen. Take a final look around, there may be other things in there, but they are outside the scope of this book. The next important thing is to learn about kitchen workshop practice.

1. THE KITCHEN WORKSHOP
What's in the tool crib

SAFETY FIRST

During the tour of the kitchen you probably noticed that the kitchen is not endowed with normal workshop safety features, and would not pass a normal plant safety inspection. There is little or no personal protection unless you provide it with a little common sense. There are no safety glasses in a box at the door, equipment has very little in the way of protective guards, and there are no Ministry Inspectors to inspect the wrong things. Safety is up to you. A few points to remember (I've forgotten the others):

> Don't move pots of boiling water or hot food around with small children in the kitchen.

> Don't try to clean rotating equipment (blenders, mixers, shredders, etc.) without stopping them first.

> Don't put metal objects inside the toaster to free jammed toast unless you have unplugged it.

> Don't use equipment which gives you a shock, even if its "only a tingle." It's broken; put it on the work bench.

> Don't turn the microwave oven on with nothing inside it. This is not a hazard to you, but it doesn't do the microwave much good. Always keep a glass of water in there when it's not in use, just in case.

> Always be prepared for fire. Baking soda can be used to extinguish oven fires. A burning pan of fat can be smothered with a lid. Keep a small fire extinguisher handy, and read the instructions before the fire starts. If none of this works immediately, get everybody out of the house at once and call the fire department from a neighbour's house. Remember the fire department are professionals.

> Always use something firm to stand on to reach those high cupboards, a chair or step-stool is best. Try to avoid using the family pet for this purpose; no matter how big it is, you'll find it very unstable.

Now that you're convinced to stay out of the kitchen forever because it's too dangerous, let's get on with the task at hand which is to help you learn how to work in there.

WORKSHOP PRACTICE

The kitchen is like any other workshop and there are some basic guidelines to follow when using the facilities. Always clean up as you go: that way you avoid finding out how strong a glue carrot soup is. If you spill something wipe it up before it dries. Also never use a cooking pot twice without cleaning between use. I tried that once. I boiled some milk, and then used the same pan again to boil some more. The result was burnt milk and a very annoyed landlady. It took a long time to clean the pan afterwards, and a much longer time to pacify the landlady.

This book uses terminology which you can understand, in preference to terms like utensils, since utensils are in fact kitchen tools. Always use the right tool for the job, and use a cutting board when using kitchen knives to avoid damaging the counter top. When using a knife, cut away from your fingers or hand. Remember kitchen knives are sharp and can easily damage your sensitive digital equipment. Take the same precautions that you would with any sharp workshop tool.

Hand Tools

Some of the basic hand tools available to the kitchen engineer are shown in Figure 1. Don't be confused by the shape, appearances can be deceptive. For example, the tool that looks like a trowel is a cake lifter, and the long bladed palette knife is used as a trowel. Cake lifters are used for serving cakes and pies after they are cooked. The kitchen spoon is a large spoon which can transport a greater volume of food than a normal table spoon. The slotted spoon is the same thing with holes in it. The holes are there to allow fluid to drain before transporting the contents.

The device which looks like a fly swatter can be used for that (when

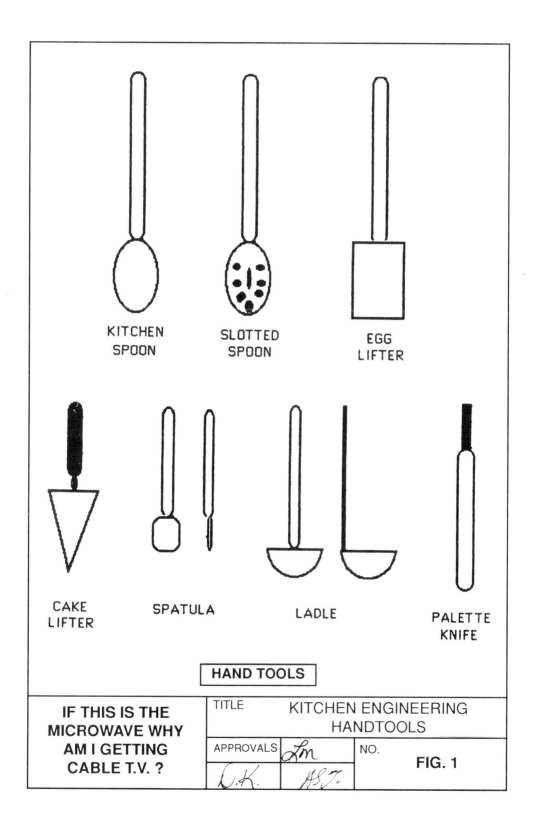

KITCHEN
SPOON

SLOTTED
SPOON

EGG
LIFTER

CAKE
LIFTER

SPATULA

LADLE

PALETTE
KNIFE

HAND TOOLS

IF THIS IS THE MICROWAVE WHY AM I GETTING CABLE T.V. ?	TITLE	KITCHEN ENGINEERING HANDTOOLS	
	APPROVALS		NO.
			FIG. 1

dirty) but is also used to lift objects like cooked eggs and fish in one piece out of a pan (when clean). The spatula is used to scrape food from the sides of bowls during mixing, and the shape of the ladle allows it to take a full level of fluid, such as soup, from a deep bowl.

The following is a list of basic tools which you may need for working in the kitchen:

- several different-sized bowls for mixing food in
- at least one sharp knife
- a vegetable peeler
- a cutting or chopping board
- scissors
- bandages
- condoms (great for keeping cut fingers dry)
- a large-size cooking spoon
- a slotted spoon
- several large and small spoons
- a wooden kitchen spoon
- a set of measuring cups
- a measuring jug with metric, ounce and cup units
- a grater — this is used for shaving or filing bits off food
- an egg lifter
- a vegetable peeler
- a spatula
- a palette knife
- a potato masher.
- a colander — this is a large bowl full of holes through which liquids or other fluids can escape, although some are reported to have difficulty deciding which hole to exit by.

Power Tools

Power tools are used in the kitchen in the same way they are at work, carefully. It's always a good idea to check the operating instructions which came with each one, if you can still find them, since this is the best way to find out how each appliance should be used. Frequently kitchen tools are used incorrectly (rolling pins are not always used for rolling pastry, for example). If all else fails look for the instructions in the C drawer providing you have several days to spare. As a last resort visit a store which sells the particular appliance and ask for a demonstration of the latest model. After a three hour demonstration tell them that you will think about it. I can assure you that sales staff have a deep affection for people who provide such an interesting interruption in the days activities, and if you look back over your shoulder as you leave you will see their lips forming silent prayers for your well-being.

During your inventory of the kitchen you have probably found:

- A toaster
- An electric kettle
- A coffee machine
- A food mixer
- A blender
- Some simple cooking devices (electric fry pan, toaster oven, crock pot etc).
- A microwave oven

I assume you already know what the toaster, electric kettle and coffee machine look like even if you may not know how to use them, so put them to one side and look at what's left over. The food mixer, if its portable, will look rather like your electric drill, but with two drill chucks instead of one. The two devices fitted to the chucks are called beaters and they counter-rotate when switched on. They are also removable for cleaning purposes. You may find that instead of, or as well as, a portable mixer you have a larger one with an attached bowl which is less portable. Experience will tell you which one to use and when.

The blender is a glass cylinder with a lid. Unplug it, take the top off and look inside; it will have small blades in the bottom which rotate at high speed when switched on. The lid is needed to stop the food from spray painting the kitchen ceiling. It is not advisable to run it with the lid off, unless you like splattered milk shake decor.

The simple cooking devices can usually be recognized by their appearance. If this fails look at the label which probably has a brief description like 'toaster oven', 'crock pot' or 'slow cooker' printed on it.

The microwave oven you have probably already met. It looks like a TV, but the picture is bad. It can cook (zap) food quickly in a serving dish, and there are no pots and pans to clean afterwards.

You now have an idea of the tools available to assist you in food preparation and it is timely to start learning how they are used in the kitchen. The next chapter provides a translation of kitchen jargon into straight everyday language which any househusband can understand.

2. PLANNING
They even have MRP here
UNDERSTANDING RECIPES

In the previous chapter you found the kitchen and looked at the equipment available to help you "cook a nice supper." Now take down one of the recipe books which are scattered around the house on various book shelves, open it and you will find that it is full of mumbo jumbo like:

•'cook sugar, water and corn syrup to medium ball stage' (are we talking tennis balls, footballs, or baseballs?)
•'brown onions' (where do I get brown onions? My mother always threw out onions which were brown.)
•'thoroughly cream shortening and sugar' (does this produce whipping cream or coffee cream, and does it provide a substitute for the cow?)
•'cook until top is creamy' (what happens to the bottom?)

What does it all mean? First let's translate it into simple layman's terms.

At the start of the recipe, or alongside it, you will find a list of items; this is the list of ingredients required for the recipe. In other words this is a simple parts list. The mumbo jumbo which follows the parts list is, in fact, the assembly instructions to prepare the recipe. In this book they will be called just that, the Parts List and the Assembly Instructions. A list of the kitchen tools required to assemble the recipe has also been included. This way you can check that you have everything before you begin, and you can ensure that the measuring cup you need was not left out in the children's sandbox overnight.

You will find many confusing terms in recipe books, and to help you some of the terms have been translated into language which you should understand better.

MUMBO JUMBO

afterburners   A househusband speciality. Reheated leftovers. This provides the opportunity to burn things twice.

baking   The process of using heat to convert unappetizing slop into delicious food.

batter   This is not a baseball term. It refers to a goop made from flour and water which is used to plaster over food before cooking.

beat   Nothing to do with music. It means to stir vigorously until its whole outlook is changed. (You can think about you ex-boss while doing this if you wish.)

bite-size   Small enough to be eaten by the smallest member of the family. The family dog is not considered the smallest member when assessing bite-size.

brown   Lightly frying in a pan until the outside is brown. Remember, when its brown its done; when its black its scrap.

burners   Stove heating elements. (A strange name for expert cooks to use for these devices.)

C drawer   The kitchen drawer which holds everything which the cook does not have a home for, but which may be useful some day.

cake batter   Cooking grout.

calorie   The heaviest atomic particle known to man.(1 food calorie = 130 milligrams). Has a particular affinity for cooks who frequently taste their own cooking. Househusbands are not immune! Caution flammable, can be burnt off.

clear   Some liquids when they reach a certain temperature become translucent. To cook until clear means to cook until there is an obvious change in the translucency. I hope this makes things clear.

colander	Leaky bowl.
cooking pot	A saucepan — it is not a fat cook or a recipe for cannabis.
cooking	The process of converting raw food to burnt using heat.
cream/creaming	The action of taking a number of ingredients and mixing them together until they have the consistency of peanut butter. Real cream is a poor analogy.
crock pot	An electric cooking device which cooks food slowly. It is not a reference to your mother-in-law.
dash	Run three times round the kitchen holding the container, then add 1/3 teaspoonful of the ingredient to the mixture.
ingredients	The list of parts required to assemble the recipe. The list can be varied by the cook, but not too much. I knew a cook who cooked Chicken a la King, but since there was no chicken in the freezer, she used fish.
kettle	A device for boiling water. Recipes frequently call for misuse of this device, 'boil the kettle', 'when the kettle is boiling'. If you encounter such terms remember that they refer to boiling the water, not the kettle.
leftovers	"No thank you, darling. If I eat any more I'll get fat." What remains are called leftovers.
menu	Kitchen name for sales specification.
mumbo jumbo	The confusing instructions included in every recipe to discourage househusbands from cooking.
recipe	Product assembly instructions.
religious cook	A person who prepares food so that it is either a burnt offering or a bloody sacrifice.
saucepan	Cooking pot. Saucepans vary in size and some can hold up to 6 litres of fluid. What would you do with 6 litres of sauce?
sauté	To keep all the ingredients on the move and hopping.

serve   The serve is as important with food as it is with tennis.
                   The object is to pass the item from the server's plate over
                   the table to the receiver's plate, without missing, and to
                   hope that the receiver will not return the serve back to the
                   server.

tablespoon   A medium-size spoon used for measuring and stirring
                   ingredients in recipes. Usually abbreviated to tbsp in
                   recipes. Also used when eating liquid foods, and for
                   cooks to taste exotic sauces. Never used for stirring
                   tables.

teaspoon   A small spoon used to measure and/or stir coffee, hot
                   chocolate, sauces, spices, cough medicine, etc. Can also
                   be used for eating ice cream. Rarely used for tea.
                   Frequently referred to in recipes as a tsp.

thick   When applied to sauces, it should have the consistency of
                   engine oil at -20° C. When applied to slices it means
                   between 0.125" and 0.375" (3 mm to 10 mm). The term
                   can also be applied to ex-bosses.

throw   Approach this term cautiously. Throw in some. . ?????...
                   means to put it in carefully. Some years ago my wife told
                   one of our sons to throw a couple of eggs into the pot. He
                   stood at the fridge and did just that. Strangely, they landed
                   in the pot without breaking.

to taste   'To taste' does not mean 'Sprinkle on and then you can
                   taste it'; it means add the ingredient if you prefer that
                   taste.

toss   See throw.

utensils   Kitchen hand tools.

zap/nuke   Short form for 'cook in the microwave'.

zapper   Microwave oven.

MRS. MURPHY'S LAWS

Mr. Murphy has achieved international status through his studies related to the Innate Perversity of Inanimate Objects, but little is known of the studies undertaken by his wife. Rummaging through an old C drawer in a disused farmhouse, I was fortunate to discover a scroll on which I was able to decipher some of her conclusions. Naturally I refer to this as my studies of the Dead C Scroll. Interspersed throughout this book are the ones I have been able to decipher to date.

THE MRP SYSTEM

If you have been involved with manufacturing you will know what an MRP system is (Manufacturing Runs out of Parts). In the kitchen MRP refers to Meal Recipe Planning. The last time you went to a restaurant, you were probably given a menu with several dishes to choose from, and from this you selected a meal. Think of the menu as a Product Specification, and the dishes offered as optional subassemblies which were used to provide the meal. Now that we have a language you understand, let us take a look at the requirements. Consider the following scenario: you have been given a contract to produce a product, 'Cook a Nice Supper' (CANS); if you don't believe it's a contract, try breaking it! Let's look at how to produce CANS.

Figure 2 gives a typical breakdown for a complete meal. Don't worry about how to prepare the individual items, that will come later (the worry, I mean). CANS is broken down into five separate subassemblies, Soup, Salad, Main Entrée, Dessert, and the Accessories. The Main Entrée is further broken down into the Main Dish (e.g. steak), the Vegetables, and the Sauce (e.g. ketchup). There will be a recipe for each of the sub assemblies which will have an associated parts list and assembly instructions. If the complete meal is made up from existing recipes, the entire process is simply a Build to Print exercise with the final options selected to please the customer.

With the meal selection made, each recipe parts list can be put together into an overall Bill of Materials (BOM) for CANS which can then be compared to the inventory list you made of the kitchen. Before you can build CANS you must have the raw materials at hand, and in the kitchen raw usually means just that. Read the BOM carefully and make sure that the materials called for are in stock, and are not on back order.

If you don't have the materials ask the purchasing agent to buy them. If you need parts urgently remember what used to happen at work? Now its your turn! Pick up the phone and call the delivery service. "Darling, please pick up some ??????? on your way home tonight." If all else fails go out and buy some on petty cash (you don't have anything else these days).

One simple method of ensuring that you have most of the ingredients available is to use packaged mixes. These are usually complete except for items like eggs or milk. Some cooks proudly announce that they have made everything from scratch, but I always worry about what they have scratched to get the ingredients.

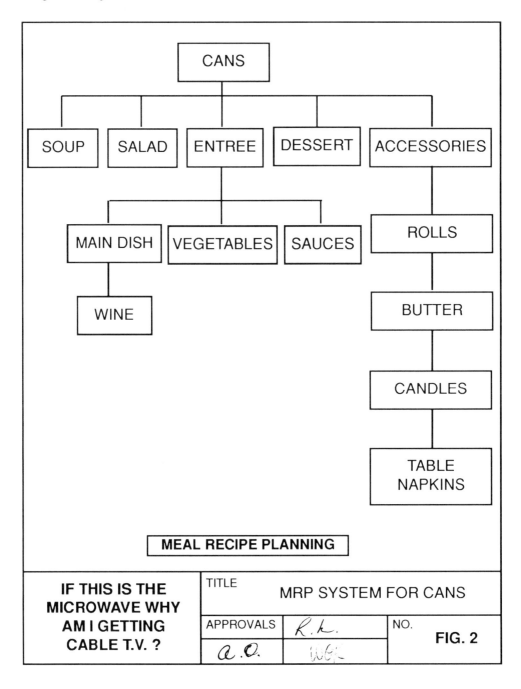

In order to finalize the BOM you need to analyze the customer requirements. Consider the size of your market. How many customers do you have? There is, of course, yourself, then how many children and how many wives? This information is necessary to determine the production batch size, and this will have an impact on the final menu selection. Don't forget to include the casual customer: "I've invited Judy to stay for supper, I hope you don't mind" (and Judy's standing right there)!

Finally you have to establish a satisfactory schedule for delivery of the end product. What time do the customers arrive, how many martinis/cokes will they need and, most important of all, when will they expect to eat?

That is meal planning in a nutshell. You can now use your vast experience gained outside the kitchen to plan the work inside the kitchen.

NUTRITION

When planning the subassemblies for CANS make sure that you provide a well balanced menu. This is quite simple if you follow the basic guidelines taught to school children and promptly forgotten. It is essential to eat a balanced diet, and this can be achieved by eating from each of the four basic food groups each day. The four groups are shown in Figure 3 and consist of:

Protein Group: Meat, fish, eggs, cheese, beans, peas, lentils, nuts, etc.

Milk Group:. Milk, cheese, ice cream and other milk-based foods.

Vegetable-Fruit Group: Dark-green or deep-yellow vegetables, citrus fruits (apples, oranges, etc.), potatoes, and other fruits and vegetables.

Bread-Cereals Group: Bread, breakfast cereals, etc.

If these foods are eaten regularly in the correct proportion, there is no need for additional supplements. Fats, sugars and flavourings can be added within the individual calorie needs and tastes.

Hold it! The magic word calorie has appeared. Everybody knows the word calorie; increase the calories and you gain weight, decrease them and you loose, right? Right! But you can burn off calories by exercise, right? Well maybe! A few years ago I took up jogging to lose weight, and I graduated to running which is a faster version of jogging, and I graduated to marathon running and I still didn't lose weight. I learnt a lot about nutrition in the process and I found out that a combination of calorie reduction and exercise is required to lose weight efficiently. I also discovered the basic rule of calories: a calorie is a calorie is a calorie. There is no such thing as a good calorie or a bad calorie. If you increase your diet by 3500 calories;

whether it be steak or cake, you will gain a pound; if you decrease it by 3500 calories you will lose a pound. Translated into practical language:

1 food calorie = +130 milligrams (added weight)

There are many good books on calorie counting and nutrition, and readers are referred to these for more information.

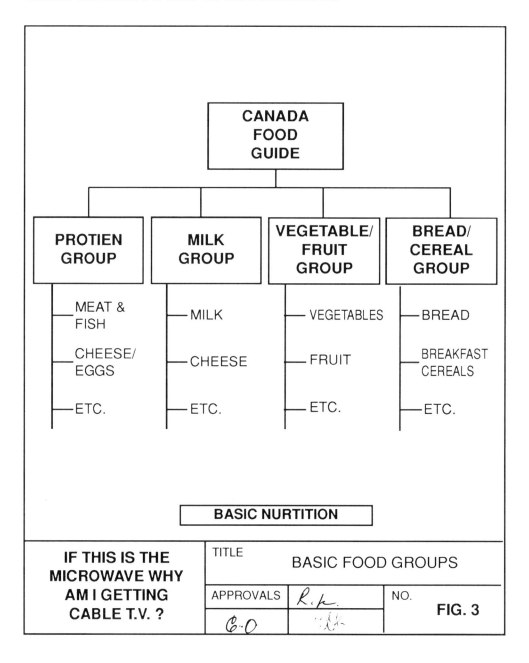

CANADA FOOD GUIDE

PROTIEN GROUP — MEAT & FISH, CHEESE/EGGS, ETC.

MILK GROUP — MILK, CHEESE, ETC.

VEGETABLE/FRUIT GROUP — VEGETABLES, FRUIT, ETC.

BREAD/CEREAL GROUP — BREAD, BREAKFAST CEREALS, ETC.

BASIC NURTITION

IF THIS IS THE MICROWAVE WHY AM I GETTING CABLE T.V. ?	TITLE	BASIC FOOD GROUPS	
	APPROVALS	R.k.	NO.
	C·O		FIG. 3

3. FOOD PREPARATION
No Problem! (if you can open the package)

The previous chapter described the kitchen environment. The next step is to learn how to transform those bags of groceries into edible food. Most food needs some preparation before it can be eaten or cooked; even oranges need peeling, apples need washing, and packages need opening, although that is a matter of personal choice. Cans should be opened before serving, and never warm up an unopened can. This chapter gives simple descriptions of basic methods of food preparation used in the kitchen.

Package Opening

Some packages are designed to be opened, others may appear to be but on closer inspection are not. Beware of packages which have little perforated lines either on the side, or on the front. Don't assume that the package should be opened at the perforation. Instructions to that effect are meant to lull you into a false sense of security. Frequently the perforation means 'crush package here'. No amount of pressure will cause the package to open at that point. Other packages state 'to open read directions'. I have spent many hours reading such directions and have never yet seen a package open by reading the directions.

If you succeed in opening the outer layer of the package by ripping the box apart, you will encounter a layer of impervious foil or plastic which resists all further attempts to open. Try pulling the seal apart; and if this doesn't work attack it with scissors. At this point you will find that you've opened the package from the bottom. This is not a problem if you are going to use all the package, but if it's something like rice or sugar, you are in trouble. I can guarantee that after you put the package back in the cupboard upside down, someone will reverse it. Remember, wipe up spills immediately.

Cans have their own unique opening problems. They frequently have lips which do not match your can opener, or they have special keys which break when you try to use them. It's difficult to open cans with scissors, but if all else fails, you could try a hack saw.

Jars and bottles come with lids which are impossible to remove by twisting. However the trick here is to bash the edge of the lid with a knife handle hard enough to dent it slightly in several places after which the lid will usually be easier to twist off.

Breaking Eggs

Eggs are individually produced in a unique package known as a shell by a machine usually referred to as a hen. Occasionally the hen makes a mistake and puts two eggs in one shell. The complete egg can be cooked in the shell, and the shell can be removed after cooking. Don't try cooking an egg this way in the microwave because it will explode; at least that's what happened to me.

Many recipes require the egg to be removed from the shell prior to use; just think of the egg as another package to open. This process is often referred to in misleading terms in recipes to confuse the unwary. Terms such as 'break the eggs into a bowl', 'put eggs into bowl', 'beat eggs into mixture' are found in many recipes and if you follow them literally you will find out the nitty gritty of cooking; the shell has to be removed first. Such expressions mean 'open the package and put the contents into the container'. This process is referred to as 'breaking the eggs'.

To break the eggs refer to Figure 4 and proceed as follows:

Break the shell in the middle of one side by striking it with a knife blade or by striking it sharply on the side of the mixing bowl. Hold the egg over a container with the cracked side down. Put the tips of both thumbs in the break and pull the shell apart as if it were hinged on the opposite side. The egg will slide out of the shell and into the container. Check that no pieces of shell have remained with the egg; if so remove them. If the recipe requires several eggs, break them into a separate bowl or cup, one at a time in case one of the eggs is bad, and then add them to the recipe (refer to Mrs. Murphy's Law #2).

Separating Eggs

This is another term used to confuse househusbands. It does not refer to putting the eggs into the separate slots in the egg carton. The egg consists of two parts, a yolk which is yellow, and a clear liquid which is called 'the white' to provide further confusion. When eggs are separated, the yolk is separated from the white. The egg white can be beaten until it becomes frothy and firm so that it retains its shape. At this point it looks rather like liquid styrofoam. The beaten egg white is used extensively in cooking for things like meringue.

The principle for separating eggs is simple. The egg is broken and the clear liquid is allowed to drain while the yellow yolk is kept separate. It is easier to separate fresh eggs at room temperature than stale eggs straight from the refrigerator. The easiest way to separate the egg is to use a special egg separator; break the egg and put the contents into the separator, the white will run out leaving the yolk behind. If you don't have a separator, the next best thing to use is a slotted kitchen spoon. Break the egg into the spoon and allow the white to run out through the holes. Some cooks break the egg into their hands and allow the white to run out through their fingers, others pour the yolk from one half of the egg shell to the other, letting the white escape. The method is not really important; the white should be separated and none of the yellow yolk must enter the mixture. If it does the egg white will not froth properly.

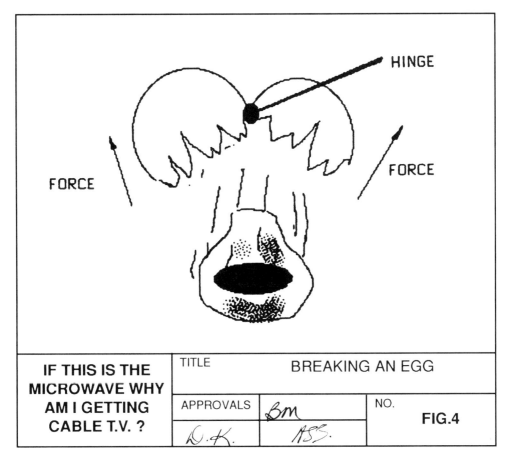

IF THIS IS THE MICROWAVE WHY AM I GETTING CABLE T.V. ?	TITLE	BREAKING AN EGG	
	APPROVALS	ℬ𝓂	NO.
	Ⅾ.K.	ASS.	FIG.4

Cutting

A lot of food is prepared by cutting; cutting techniques are especially useful for preparing fresh vegetables. Cutting is not usually required if frozen or canned food is used, providing you have found out how to open the packages. The following sections describe the terms and different cutting techniques used in food preparation.

Peeling

Peeling is the action of removing the skin of fruits or vegetables with a knife or with a special peeling tool which can be bought at most grocery stores. The idea is to remove the skin and leave as much of the object being peeled as possible. Take the object in one hand and carefully remove a thin layer of the skin with one stroke of the knife (no! not your skin, the object's). Repeat this until all the skin has been removed. Since the skin is a protective coating and most things go brown quickly after peeling, it is advisable to peel items just before use and not the day before. To reduce the browning effect immerse the item in water after peeling.

Peeling is required prior to cooking fruit (apples, pears) and vegetables (carrots, parsnips, potatoes, rutabagas). For some items, e.g. oranges, a knife can be used to lift a small layer of skin which can then be pulled off.

Shredding

Shredding is the process of slicing very thin. Some appliances are equipped with blades to do the shredding for you, but a sharp knife can also be used. In the case of root vegetables like carrots and parsnips, shred them along the major axis (lengthways).

Trimming

Trimming removes all the unwanted material from the food. This would include for example, the fat from meat, and all the brown leaves and roots from vegetables like lettuce, celery, cabbage and leeks. Note that a cabbage would be trimmed before shredding.

Tearing

Some foods are best prepared by tearing them up into bite-size pieces. Lettuce for salads is frequently prepared this way. The food should be thoroughly washed before and after tearing.

Slicing

Slicing is done with a sharp knife and is used to make the food pieces smaller so that they will cook quickly and be easier to eat. It also ensures that the food is sound in the middle.

- Root vegetables are usually sliced.
- Potatoes can be sliced into halves or quarters.
- Brussels sprouts should be trimmed of outer brown leaves and then sliced in half.
- Rutabagas (Swedish turnips) create a special problem because of their size and hardness. They can be sliced into smaller pieces using a sharp knife and the slices can be peeled. After peeling, the slices can be washed and then cut into bite-size pieces. It is very difficult to cut rutabagas into halves and quarters.

Mixing

Mixing is the process of combining all the specified ingredients into one homogenized mess in the order given in the recipe. The recipe will specify whether the mixing is done dry or wet. Dry mixing uses no liquid and will generate clouds of dust if attempted with the mixer on too high a speed. Start slowly and increase speed if necessary.

The problem with wet mixing is to know how much wet to add. Usually the required mix consistency is that of wet cement prior to pouring, so if you can remember how the cement looked when you poured that patio last summer, then you have it right. Start a wet mix the same way you would for cement; make a small mound of the dry ingredients in the mixing bowl, put a hole in the centre, and pour the liquid into the hole. Fold and mix with a spoon, spatula or fork instead of a shovel. You can also use a power mixer for larger quantities just as you did for the cement. Strangely enough; if you mix it properly the baking will not be as hard as cement.

Cooking

There are many ways of applying heat to food and if you are lucky some of them will work for you. Among the methods of heating food are:

Boiling / simmering	Baking
Toasting	Roasting
Broiling	Microwaving
Frying	Slow cooking

Boiling, Simmering

Boiling is the process of cooking food in boiling water until it is soft or otherwise cooked. Some foods, like eggs, start off soft and become hard through boiling.

Simmering is a slightly different form of boiling in which the food is held close to the boiling point. During simmering, very small bubbles are produced around the edges of the pan rather than the more vigorous bubbling associated with boiling.

Toasting

Toasting is the action of putting food close to a red hot surface so that it will brown nicely. It is very useful for snacks.

Broiling

Broiling is a more advanced form of toasting in which the food is placed under the red hot surface to cook. Broiling is usually done in a stove fitted with a broiling element and is a sort of indoor barbecuing. It is sometimes referred to as grilling.

Frying

Frying is the process of applying heat directly to the food with a pan or skillet. A small quantity of fat is used in the pan to prevent the food from sticking. Some foods, like bacon, have natural fat which is extracted by the heat.

Baking, Roasting

Baking and **roasting** are performed in the oven. Items to be baked or roasted are put in the oven at a temperature between 300° and 500° F until they are cooked. The recipe will tell you whether you are baking or roasting, and what temperature to use.

Microwaving

The **microwave** oven is very useful for preparing meals quickly, or for afterburners (reheated leftovers). Microwaves apply heat more efficiently than a conventional stove, and they use less electrical power. The reason for their efficiency is that the heat is applied from the inside to the outside, unlike conventional cooking in which the outside of the food is heated and the heat must find its own way to the middle to finish cooking. The main disadvantage with the microwave is that food doesn't brown and can look somewhat unappetizing even if cooked properly. Microwave recipes usually get around this by covering the food up with a sauce or icing in much the same way as paint is used to cover rusty auto body parts.

Slow Cooking

The slow cooker is a ceramic pot which is heated electrically from a metal jacket. The pot is covered and the heat can be set so that the pot simmers safely for long periods of time. It is very useful to the househusband because foods can be left cooking all day when he goes for job interviews, or out to play golf, and he can still provide CANS when the wife gets home.

Slow cooking is not restricted to slow cookers; any recipe for a slow cooker can be cooked in a large cooking pot, but the pot must not be left unattended in case it burns, or cools off.

Flavourings

A chapter on food preparation would not be complete without a mention of the flavourings used in cooking. These are not to be confused with the store bought Sauces and Relishes (SAR) which are frequency used in large quantities to hide the flavour of the food. When this happens you have to go on a SAR (Search and Rescue) mission to find out what you are eating.

Flavourings can be classified in two categories for this book, Seasonings and Liquids.

Seasonings

Seasonings are to cooking what a tune-up is to your automobile engine—it may not be necessary, but you can sure tell the difference when it is done.

Two basic seasonings are salt and pepper which are usually available on most meal tables so that diners can flavour food to suit their own tastes. Seasonings are usually strong flavoured or flavour inducing herbs and spices which are added in small quantities during cooking. The quantity added is very much a matter of taste, and the recipe amount is only a suggested quantity. Trial and error will help you determine what to do. If you like it salty, add a little more, if you are on a salt-free diet, leave it out, and the same goes for other seasonings.

One problem for the beginning cook is to know what seasonings are available and what taste change will result. The following list gives some of the more common ones and provides an indication of the taste effect. Some seasonings appeal to the sense of smell, and are used to improve the aroma of the food. "Boy that smells good." Seasonings which have aroma are listed as fragrant.

Fragrant and fruity: Tarragon, cinnamon, allspice. Cinnamon, of course supplies the flavour and aroma of cinnamon buns.

Fragrant and bitter: Oregano, bay leaves, sage, rosemary, nutmeg, cloves. Nutmeg is frequently used to flavour pumpkin pie.

Fresh and slightly sweet: Mint, parsley, celery, paprika.

Hot: Black pepper, white pepper, mustard, chili powder, horseradish.

Licorice (faint): Anise, caraway, dill.

Mild: Marjoram, sweet basil, thyme, savory, mace.

Onion: Onions, garlic. (One would hardly call the smell of garlic fragrant.)

Oriental: Curry powder, cumin seeds, ginger.

This gives a cross section of some of the seasonings available. Check what you have in the cupboards against the list; it is a good idea to have one or two from each group to start with, for example pepper and chili powder from the hot group.

Liquids

There are many liquid flavourings used in cooking and they vary from concentrated essences like vanilla to alcoholic beverages like beer and wine. Many recipes call for the use of alcoholic beverages, but the beer or wine is only added for the flavour. The cooking action evaporates the alcohol quite quickly. This is the reason why coffee served with liqueur is topped with whipped cream. The thick layer of cream prevents the alcohol from evaporating.

Also available at the supermarket are many concentrated liquid flavourings in little bottles. Many of the names provide familiar tastes. It is sometimes better to use a rum flavouring rather than pure rum because the flavouring gives a more authentic taste than the real thing after cooking.

Typical flavourings include:

Concentrated Peppermint, almond, maple, rum, brandy, orange and vanilla.

Alcoholic Beer, wine, spirits, liqueurs.

Sauces Tabasco, tomato, Worcester.

Fruit juices Lemon, orange, grapefruit.

Two words which are used frequently in recipes are Marinate and Macerate.

Marinate originally meant to pickle in brine (marine, sea) but is used today to indicate soaking meat or fish in a heavily spiced liquid for several hours prior to cooking. The liquid base can be wine, lemon juice, brine or anything which will impart a distinctive flavour to the flesh. The recipe will indicate which marinade to use.

Macerate, on the other hand, means to soften by soaking, and the term is frequently applied to fruits soaked in a flavoured sugar solution or liqueur.

SUMMARY

This chapter has given you a simple introduction to preparing food for cooking. It has discussed opening packages, including eggs, and has described the basic techniques for getting food ready. The different methods of cooking have been described, and finally the importance of flavourings has been mentioned. That's it! Time for a coffee break.

MRS. MURPHY'S LAW #1

The watched pot never boils.
Corollary: The unwatched pot always burns.

---

4. PROTOTYPES
Nobody minds if you make mistakes

O.K! Coffee break is over, it's time to put on your work boots, safety glasses, oven mitts and hard hat and get to work.

The previous chapters have given a general introduction to the kitchen. You have found out where it is, what is in it, what the equipment is used for, how to prepare food, and you should have made a parts inventory. You are now ready to start experimenting with some simple prototype recipes which will teach you how to use the equipment. There is always some experimentation required when cooking. Food is rarely cooked in standard units, you cannot buy a standard carrot, and even if you could, ovens, burners and cookers vary according to size, power and manufacture. Let's face it, autos from different manufacturers behave differently so why shouldn't stoves. Be prepared to experiment all the time; if your oven cooks slower than the recipe specifies then always add that little extra time; if it's too hot at the required setting, turn it down. Cooking is not a precise science.

Please bear in mind that prototypes are not for delivery to your customers, but may be shown to them to establish credibility. On occasion potential customers may be permitted to evaluate a sample but only if it will further establish your credibility as a cook. Remember, evaluation by the customer is not always offered free of charge. It's nice to persuade somebody else to wash the dishes.

The prototype recipes are simple and use only one mixture and method of heating so that you can learn the basic first principles and become familiar with your equipment. Most of the recipes make good lunchtime snacks and can be eaten or thrown out before the family comes home so they won't be aware of failures. "Dad burnt the toast again." Experiment a little, but don't burn the house down or you will probably ruin your entire day, and it won't do your ego much good either.

PROTOTYPE RECIPES

It is not necessary to cook food to prepare a meal. Salads and fruit make excellent cold snacks or meals. This first recipe does not need any cooking.

Grapefruit

A friend has just returned from Florida and with a grin has given you a nice fresh grapefruit. (He doesn't know what to do with it either.) It's simple.

Parts List

> 1 Grapefruit
> Sugar to taste
> 1 Maraschino Cherry

Tools Required

> 1 grapefruit knife or any small sharp knife

Assembly Instructions

The grapefruit is constructed like an orange with a peel and segments. The object is to cut the grapefruit in half across the segments so that the skin forms a dish with the half segments inside.

Look at the grapefruit carefully; you will see two marks, one where the fruit was attached to the tree and the other diametrically opposite. Pick a point on the skin half way between these two marks and using a sharp knife, cut the grapefruit in half. You should now have two sections in which the segments radiate out from the centre like a star as shown in Figure 5.

It is easier to do the next step with a grapefruit knife if you have one. Note the location of the segment separations and cut along each one of these from the middle to the skin, but do not cut through the outside skin. Next, cut around the outside of the segments so that you separate the segments from the outer skin.

You now have a half grapefruit with individual segments for easier eating with a spoon. Sprinkle sugar on top to taste and put a maraschino cherry in the centre. The maraschino cherry is added for style and appearance. (Don't forget your marketing training while in the kitchen. Making food look attractive to eat is very important.)

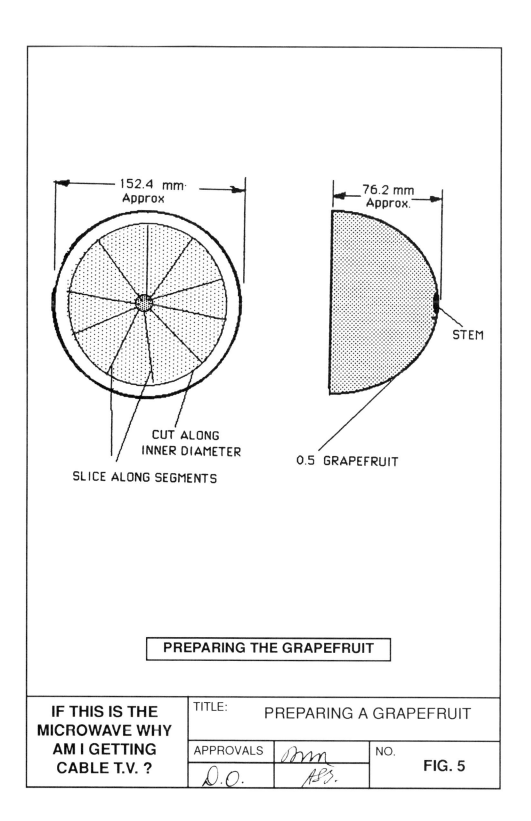

152.4 mm. Approx

76.2 mm Approx.

STEM

CUT ALONG INNER DIAMETER

SLICE ALONG SEGMENTS

0.5 GRAPEFRUIT

PREPARING THE GRAPEFRUIT

IF THIS IS THE MICROWAVE WHY AM I GETTING CABLE T.V. ?	TITLE: PREPARING A GRAPEFRUIT	
	APPROVALS	NO.
	D.O.	FIG. 5

Coffee

Some people have the mistaken impression that men who go out to work each day are incapable of even boiling water. They have the illusion that their wife gets breakfast, their secretary makes all the coffee, and they eat out at business lunches. These people believe that men who don't have secretaries and business lunches nevertheless have cafeterias, coffee shops or mobile canteens which supply their needs. Now we all know that this is wrong, but just in case there is an exception out there (and I doubt it), the next two recipes cover coffee and tea making. If you know how to do this take a coffee break while everybody else catches up to you. If you don't drink coffee, then pretend. We'll be back in about half an hour.

For those of you who have stayed you will need the following:

Parts List

> Ground coffee to suit coffee machine
> Water as required
> Sugar, cream, whitener, liquor as desired.

Tools Required

> Coffee machine (drip or percolator)
> Measuring spoon

When you have everything together and are ready, then follow the instructions.

Assembly Instructions

Measure the required quantity of water into the coffee maker, i.e. how many people want coffee and how many cups do *you* want? Put the coffee filter into the basket if your system uses one. Measure the required number of spoonfuls of ground coffee and put them into the basket or filter funnel. If you don't know how much coffee to use, you can try 1 heaped teaspoon for every two cups of water, and then adjust the quantity to suit next time you make coffee.

Plug in and turn on the coffee machine. When it has finished its cycle (the light has come on, or it's stopped dripping, — whatever), pour into cups or mugs and add sugar and cream to taste, just like at work.

Keep trying until you are satisfied with the taste.

Tea

Tea is a refreshing drink which should not be confused with the meal (Afternoon Tea). We are not concerned with Afternoon Tea here. This recipe requires you to boil water in a kettle. Tea can be made by throwing a tea bag into a cup of hot water, but that ignores the finer things of making tea and the water still has to be boiled. Tea has formed the basis for protocol in many countries. I recall being on a British Airways flight out of Heathrow, England on which the Captain announced "We will be ready to take-off when everyone has finished tea"(!) and we waited until everyone had finished.

To make a good cup of tea proceed as follows:

Parts List

1 packet of tea bags or loose tea
Water as required.
Milk, sugar, lemon etc. to taste

Tools Required

1 kettle
1 teapot (with a vent hole in the lid)
1 teaspoon (what else would you use)
Kitchen tongs (if using tea bags)
Tea strainer (if using loose tea)

Assembly Instructions

Pour enough water in the kettle to make sufficient cups of tea. If the water overflows you need a bigger kettle. Plug in and turn on the kettle to boil the water, and just before the water boils put the teapot near the kettle. Pour a small amount of water into the teapot. This is used to warm up the teapot. Tea should always be made in a warm pot.

Pour the water out when the pot is warm, and then add either the tea bags or spoonfuls of loose tea. Tea strength is very much a matter of taste, and if you are unsure on your first attempt, try one spoon or tea bag for every 2 cups for an average-size teapot.

Some kettles are fitted with devices which tell you when the water is boiling. If you don't have this luxury, look for large quantities of steam coming from the spout. When the water is boiling, pour it into the teapot until the pot is full, then replace the teapot lid. At this point, if the lid does not have a vent hole, the tea will pour out of the spout when the air inside the lid expands with the heat.

Let the teapot stand for a few minutes; this is known as letting the tea steep. Pour the tea into cups and serve with milk, sugar or lemon with due ceremony, particularly before take-off. If you used loose tea, use a tea strainer to filter out the tea leaves when pouring into the cups.

Toast

Toast is very simple to make, particularly if you have an automatic toaster. If the toaster is on your workbench to be fixed, toast can also be made using the broiling element on the oven. It requires a source of red hot heat, so don't try making it in the microwave.

Parts List

> 1 or 2 slices of bread
> Butter, margarine, jam, peanut butter, etc. to taste

Tools Required

> Toaster or broiler
> Knife

Assembly Instructions

Toaster: Place the bread in the toaster and turn it on. Keep an eye on it to make sure that the toast does not burn, and that the toaster switches off.

Broiler: Put the oven rack at its highest position, turn the broiler to high, and place the bread so that it is close to the red element. Watch carefully, and when it turns brown, remove it, turn it over and repeat for the other side. Handle carefully, it will be hot.

When the toast is done, spread a thin layer of butter or margarine on one side, and add your favourite jam, marmalade or other topping.

MRS. MURPHY'S LAW #2

The last egg broken into the bowl is always bad.

Hot Soup

This recipe uses the elements (burners) on the stove top for cooking, and teaches the technique of simmering. Tinned soup can be heated on the stove to make a quick meal and partial instructions for cooking are usually printed on the label. Proceed as follows:

Parts List

>   10 oz (284 mL) tin of soup
>   Water or milk if required by the recipe on the can

Tools Required

>   Gas or electric stove
>   Saucepan to hold contents of soup can
>   Large spoon for stirring
>   Can opener

Assembly Instructions

Read the instructions on the can to determine if liquid should be added to the soup. Open the can with the can opener, being careful not to cut yourself on the sharp edges of the lid.

Pour the contents into the saucepan, add the liquid if required and stir to blend with the soup. Put the saucepan on the stove and turn the heat to medium or medium high. If the heat is too high it may cause the soup to burn on the bottom of the pan.

Stir as the soup is warming until it comes to the boil and then turn the heat down until it is just simmering. When it boils the surface becomes quite agitated, when it is simmering, small bubbles appear where the soup touches the edges of the pan. Simmer for 2 to 3 minutes, watching carefully to see that it doesn't suddenly boil over, then transfer into individual bowls using a ladle or large spoon. Be very careful, hot soup retains heat longer than water.

MRS. MURPHY'S LAW #3

A package opened from the bottom is self-righting.

Boiled Egg

Some recipes call for food to be boiled. This is the process of keeping the liquid in a cooking pot at its boiling point until the cooking process is complete. Many liquids can be boiled, for example milk, water, soups and sauces. The skill lies in maintaining the water at boiling point without either boiling the pot dry, boiling too vigorously so that the liquid overflows, or burning the pot. If the liquid stops boiling the food may not cook properly. In the previous recipe the soup was brought to the boil and the heat was then turned down to simmer it. The next step is to practise bringing something to the boil and keeping it there. For this we will boil an egg.

Parts List

> 1 fresh egg
> Water as required
> Salt and pepper to taste

Tools Required

> Saucepan deep enough to cover the egg when water is added
> Spoon or kitchen tongs
> Egg cup
> Tea spoon
> Clock or egg timer

Assembly Instructions

Put enough water in the pot to ensure that the egg will be covered. Do not add the egg at this stage. Turn the heat control for the element to high and bring the water to a vigorous boil. Gently place the egg in the boiling water using the spoon or tongs, and start the timer. The water will probably stop boiling for a few seconds due to the cold egg, but should resume boiling almost immediately. Turn the heat down slightly, and watch to see that the water remains boiling.

Leave the egg in the water for three to five minutes (three minutes if it is to be soft boiled and runny, and five minutes for hard boiled). The time can be varied for all points in between to suit personal preferences.

When the time has elapsed, use the spoon or tongs to remove the egg from the boiling water and place it in the egg cup for serving. Serve with slices of bread and butter or margarine, and add salt and pepper to suit individual tastes.

Omelette

Frying is a popular way to prepare food and is used a lot in recipes to add a brown tinge to meats and vegetables for flavour and appearance. That is what the term 'brown' refers to in recipes. In this recipe, frying will be used as the complete cooking process.

Parts List

> 2 fresh eggs
> 2 tablespoons (30 mL) milk
> Cooking oil or butter as preferred (Margarine does not brown well which may affect the food's appearance.)
> Pepper and salt to taste

Tools Required

> Small frying pan
> Small mixing bowl
> Fork or egg whisk
> Egg lifter

Assembly Instructions

Break the eggs and put the contents in the bowl. Add the milk and beat the mixture with the fork or whisk with a vigorous back and forth motion until the milk and eggs are blended into a smooth mixture. (An electric mixer could be used for this if preferred.)

Turn the stove element to high. Add sufficient cooking oil to the frying pan to provide just a thin film of oil over the bottom of the pan. This will stop the mixture from sticking to the hot pan. Heat the pan until the oil begins to smoke slightly, then pour in the beaten mixture. The mixture should spread over the bottom of the pan and will sizzle slightly until the pan cools.

The mixture will begin to cook at the edges of the pan; the heat should be turned down to medium at this point. Use the egg lifter to move the cooked portions away from the edges and tilt the pan slightly to allow more liquid to contact the edges. When no more liquid will flow because it is all solid, use the egg lifter and lifting one side of the omelette, fold it in half. Continue cooking on one side, lifting the edge frequently to ensure that it is not burning. When it is brown on that side, turn the omelette over and brown the other side.

Remove the omelette and serve with bread and butter.

. . . continued on page 48

The omelette recipe can be varied by adding other items to the mixture before cooking such as 0.5 cup of grated cheese, ham cut into small pieces, tomato pieces or a small (1 teaspoon) amount of savoury flavourings. Try it, that's what prototyping is all about.

Muffins

The previous recipes covered the techniques of boiling, simmering, broiling and frying. This recipe uses the oven to bake some muffins. There are some excellent muffin mixes available which contain most or all of the ingredients, and they are almost foolproof. (Nothing is foolproof; fools are very ingenious). The instructions given here are only typical for a muffin mix. They are based on certain mixes and if your mix has different instructions follow them. A muffin pan is required for this recipe; details of a typical muffin pan are given in Figure 6.

Parts List

> 1 packet of muffin mix
> Ingredients as called for with the mix
> (1 egg, cooking oil, milk, etc.).
> Water as required

Tools Required

> Medium-size mixing bowl
> Muffin pan for 12 muffins (teflon coated preferred)
> Packet of large paper baking cups
> Fork
> Tablespoon
> Measuring cups
> Oven mitts

Assembly Instructions

Read the instructions with the mix. Check that the oven is empty, and that there is a suitable shelf in the middle to put the muffins on. Set the oven switch to 'bake' and turn it on to the temperature specified on the packet. This will allow the oven to heat up while the muffins are being mixed. Make sure the oven has not been put on broil by mistake.

Measure the correct amount of mix into the bowl. Put all the specified liquids, i.e. water, eggs, milk, cooking oil, into a small bowl and mix thoroughly with the fork. Add the liquid mix to the muffin mix, in the same way that you would add water to cement, and mix everything together using the fork until all liquid has been absorbed by the mix. Do not use a power mixer for muffins. The final mix may look lumpy, but this is alright.

Put the baking cups into the muffin pan, using one for each space. Use the tablespoon to put some of the mixture into each baking cup and divide the amounts equally between the cups. Use all the mix; the cups should be about 2/3 full.

Check that the oven is up to temperature; if it's not wait until it is, then put the muffin pan on the shelf in the middle of the oven. Be careful, the oven is hot! Close the oven door. Set the oven timer to five minutes less than the specified cooking time. When the time is up, check the muffins. They should be larger than when they were put in, but they will probably still look moist on top in the middle. Continue cooking for a few minutes until the tops of the muffins are golden brown all over. Remember, when they are brown they are done, if they are black they are scrap.

Put on oven mitts. No! Not the flowery ones hanging on the wall, use the ones with the burnt edges in the drawer. If you can't find those you can always use your baseball mitt and a cloth. Be careful, everything will be hot. Remove the pan from the oven and place it on a heat resistant surface to cool. Turn the oven off.

Leave the muffins to cool for 15 minutes, then carefully put a blunt edge under the side of each one, lever up and the cup should just pop out. Transfer to a plate, and leave to cool further.

When you have baked a few mixes successfully, try experimenting. In many muffin mixes, the flavouring ingredient, e.g. raisins, carrots, or banana, is usually weak. It is quite OK to add an extra quantity of these at the mixing stage. Put in an extra handful of raisins, grate up a small carrot, or mash up half a banana with a fork. It certainly improves the flavour. Try sprinkling brown sugar on top of carrot muffins before putting them in the oven. With these innovations you will soon produce high-grade muffins.

MRS. MURPHY'S LAW #4

There will always be one item less in the cupboard than the recipe requires.

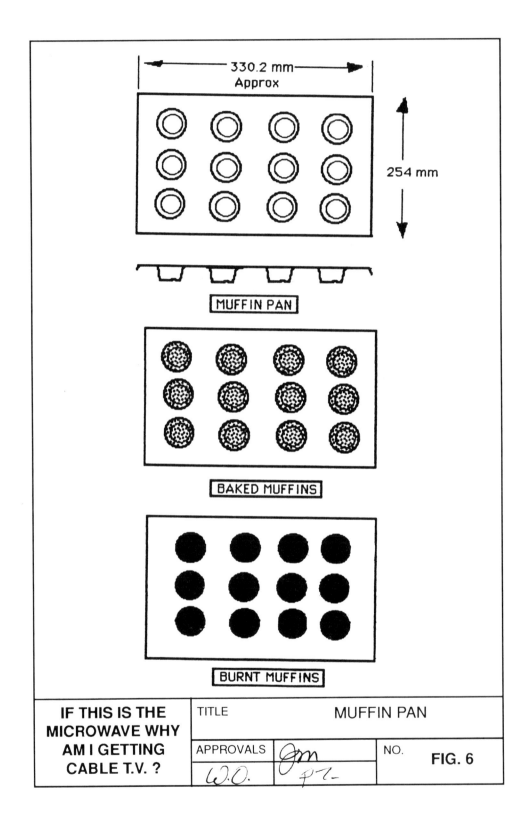

330.2 mm Approx

254 mm

MUFFIN PAN

BAKED MUFFINS

BURNT MUFFINS

IF THIS IS THE MICROWAVE WHY AM I GETTING CABLE T.V. ?	TITLE	MUFFIN PAN	
	APPROVALS		NO. FIG. 6

Microwave Cake

Microwave ovens are quick, and they use normal dishes, so there are no dirty saucepans to clean. Once again we will use a mix, this time to bake a cake. It was mentioned earlier that the microwave does not brown food and that microwave recipes usually use something to hide this fact. With cakes the final product is iced to achieve the desired effect; just like any other production, you apply a final finish to make the product look good for the customer.

Parts List

1 cake mix suitable for microwave cooking
Eggs and other liquids as required by the recipe

Tools Required

Medium-size mixing bowl
Measuring cups
Microwave cake pan (sometimes this is included with the package)
Fork or cake whisk
Tablespoon
Palette knife or broad-bladed knife

Assembly Instructions

Follow the instructions on the package. If they don't make sense, then read on. Open the package and put the dry cake mix in the mixing bowl. Put the other liquids and the eggs (after emptying them from the shell) into a separate container and beat by hand using a fork or egg beater.

Make a mound of the dry mix with a hole in the top as for mixing cement, and pour the liquid in. Blend the mixture with the water using the fork in place of a shovel. The final consistency of the grout should be about the same as a cement mix—smooth with no lumps. The grout obtained when mixing cakes is called cake batter. Transfer the cake batter to the cake pan and spread it flat using the back of a spoon and a trowel-like motion to push it into the corners. Don't try to make it too flat, the baking will modify the shape because cakes rise in the middle.

Place the cake batter and pan in the microwave oven and zap it at the power level and time specified in the cake mix instructions. Check to see if the cake is done by gently pushing on it. If your finger sinks in and comes out sticky, the cake is not done. Zap it at the same power for a further 30 seconds. If the cake bounces back when pushed, it is done. Take the cake from the oven and allow it to cool.

Follow the mix instructions for making the icing, and apply it to the top surface of the cool cake. Trowel it over the surface with the palette knife to give a smooth even finish. This time you can show your professional expertise and try fancy techniques if you wish, however don't expect as smooth a finish as you would get with plaster. Also, you won't be able to sand it smooth when it's dry.

The Super Bowl

(Serves 6.) This recipe is ideal for the sports enthusiastic since it takes only a few minutes to prepare and a long time to cook. This way you can watch the game while the meal cooks, just checking occasionally during the game breaks or commercials. The final result resembles Chili Con Carne, and it is prepared in the slow cooker.

Parts List

1 lb (450 gm) ground lean beef
2 onions
1 green pepper
2 or 3 celery stalks
1 10 oz (284 mL)can tomato soup
1 14 oz (398 mL)can red kidney beans
1 to 3 tbsp (5-15 mL) chili powder
2 cups (500 mL) tomato ketchup

Tools Required

Slow cooker
Sharp knife
Can opener
Tablespoon
Wooden cooking spoon
Television set tuned to sports channel
Liquid refreshments to taste

Assembly Instructions

Peel and slice the onions into rings and then cut the rings in half. Slice and chop up the green pepper into 1/4" (6 mm) square pieces, taking care to remove all the pepper seeds. Wash the celery and slice it up into small, 1/2" (12 mm) long pieces; if the leaves are fresh and green they can be included. If you require instructions on preparing the vegetables, turn to the Field Support section.

Put the ground beef into the slow cooker. Add the chopped vegetables. Open the cans of soup and kidney beans and add these to the cooker. Put in the tomato ketchup. Sprinkle the chili powder over the top of the mixture. If you like it mild, try one tablespoon; if you like it hot, try two; and if you think you know hot chili, try three. Stir and mix lightly with the wooden spoon. Put the lid on the slow cooker and turn the heat to high.

Turn on the television, open the liquid refreshments and relax. At the end of the first period, quarter, set, etc., check the pot to see how things are cooking. Stir to mix all ingredients, replace the lid and return to the game. Repeat for each interval. The total cooking time is about six hours on high.

An alternative to watching television is to stir after cooking on high for one hour, turn the crock pot to low, and leave for a round of golf.

Serve in bowls with bread and butter. When you have graduated to the mature product level, you can also serve it with a salad.

Quick Chili

Chili taste improves with the time allowed for cooking. However, if you are on the seventh hole when you remember that you forgot to make the chili, all is not lost. You can use the same parts as for the Super Bowl but modify the assembly procedure and use an extra tablespoon (15 mL) of chili powder. You will need a frying pan and a deep pot with a lid.

Prepare the vegetables as before. Put the frying pan on the stove, add two tablespoons of cooking oil, and turn the heat to medium high. Put the onions, pepper, and celery into the frying pan and fry them until they are cooked, using a spoon to turn them frequently to prevent burning. When they are cooked, sprinkle the chili powder onto the mixture, add the beef and mix it in with the vegetables. Continue frying until the beef is nice and brown, then remove the pan from the heat.

Transfer the beef and vegetable mixture to the deep cooking pot. Open the cans of tomato soup and kidney beans, and add the contents to the mixture. Add the ketchup and stir thoroughly. Put the pot back on the stove and bring the contents to the boil over a medium-high heat, stirring frequently to prevent burning, then turn the heat down to medium low. Put the lid on the pot and simmer for 15 minutes. Adjust the heat if necessary. The chili can then be served as before, and you are off the hook.

SUMMARY

In this chapter the basics of cooking have been covered without, I hope, a very religious overtone. The following has been accomplished. We have learnt how to:

Boil water in a kettle.
Use a coffee machine.
Make toast using the broiler.
Simmer something on the stove.
Boil something on the stove.
Bake in the oven.
Bake in the microwave.
Use a slow cooker (crock pot).

The recipes in the next chapter are for simple meals using these basics.

MRS. MURPHY'S LAW #5

The arrival of visitors turns milk sour.

---

5. DEVELOPMENT MODELS
Time to start getting serious

If you have survived the previous chapter without burning the house down, and you have produced edible products which you could eat, then you now know how to cook. You can now turn your attention to recipes which involve more than one method of cooking. This gives you the opportunity to burn things twice which is much more interesting. In preparing meals it is important that each item arrives at the table at the correct temperature; hot soup should be hot, and ice cream should be cold. It is not a good idea to leave the ice cream out while you open the soup can, pour it into the pot, warm it up and eat it, unless you like liquid ice cream. The following recipes require more than one method of cooking so that you can practise getting everything together at the right time. At work you called this scheduling.

Again these development models are not for customer consumption except on a trial basis. However if you are satisfied with the result, then you can serve it up at an appropriate time. Many simple meals can be combined with toast and the first few recipes illustrate this.

Cowboy Beans on Toast

(Feeds 2 adults or 3 or 4 small kids.) One day when my wife had delegated me as cook, the kids came in and asked "What's to eat Dad?" Not having any better idea at the time I said "Beans on toast" which was promptly greeted by loud "Yuks!!!" I thought quickly and said in my most convincing voice "Hey wait, these are different, these are cowboy beans, the ones the cowboys ate when they rounded up cattle." After a long sceptical pause at which they looked at each other, the oldest said "OK" and we had beans on toast for lunch. From then on they would only agree to beans on toast if they were cowboy beans hence this recipe.

In those days every boy strapped a six shooter on his hips, so the idea was well received. Today you might have to serve computer chips, but the idea is the same; when feeding kids learn to think on your feet or eat it all yourself. In that case the recipe feeds one fat adult.

Parts List

1 14 oz (398 mL) can baked beans
1 slice of bread per person
Butter or margarine.

Tools Required

Toaster
Small cooking pot
Can opener
Knife
Tablespoon
Serving plates

Assembly Instructions

Open the can of beans and pour the contents into the cooking pot. Add 1/4 cup (60 mL) of water and stir. Warm on the stove on medium heat, stirring continuously with the spoon, until the mixture is simmering. Turn heat to low.

Make toast using the toast recipe, and spread with butter or margarine. Put toast on serving plates. Take the pot off the stove, and use the spoon to put equal portions of the beans on each piece of toast. Turn off the stove.

Serve immediately before they change their mind!!!

Scrambled Eggs on Toast

(Serves 2 or 3.) A simple recipe which combines two of the recipes in the last chapter.

Parts List

> 2 fresh eggs
> 2 tablespoons (30 mL) of milk
> Cooking oil (optional)
> Butter
> Pepper and salt to taste
> Two or three slices of bread
> Ketchup

Tools Required

> Small frying pan
> Small mixing bowl
> Fork
> Spoon
> Toaster

Assembly Instructions

Break the eggs and put the contents in the bowl. Add the milk and beat the mixture with the fork with a vigorous back and forth motion until the milk and the eggs are blended into a smooth mixture. (An electric mixer could be used for this if preferred.) Add the pepper and salt as desired.

Put the bread in the toaster, but do not turn it on.

Turn the stove element to high. Add sufficient butter or cooking oil to the frying pan to just provide a thin film over the bottom of the pan. Heat the pan until the oil begins to smoke slightly. then pour in the beaten mixture. The mixture should spread over the bottom of the pan and will sizzle slightly until the pan cools.

Turn on the toaster.

The mixture in the pan will begin to cook at the edges of the pan. When this happens turn the heat down to medium high. At this point the process changes from making an omelette. Use the fork to stir the mixture so that it remains uniform; the mixture will gradually become less liquid and will scramble into small pieces. When the liquid has gone, but while the eggs are still moist, turn the heat off, but leave the pan on the stove. Stir in a tablespoonful of ketchup.

Remove the toast when it is done and spread it with butter or margarine. Place the toast on the serving plates, and spoon the egg from the pan onto the toast, dividing it into equal portions. Turn off the stove.

Serve immediately.

Sardines on Toast

(Serves 2 or 3.) Another simple recipe using toast.

Parts List

       1 tin (100 g) sardines
       1 fresh egg
       Cooking oil
       Butter or margarine
       Pepper and salt to taste
       2 or 3 slices of bread

Tools Required

       Small cooking pot
       Small mixing bowl
       Fork
       Spoon
       Toaster
       Can opener.

Assembly Instructions

Open the tin of sardines and put the contents in the bowl. Mash the sardines into small pieces with the fork. Break the egg and put the contents in the bowl with the sardines. Add pepper and salt as desired. Mash the egg and the sardines together until they are blended into a smooth paste.

Turn the stove element to medium. Add sufficient butter or cooking oil to the pot to just provide a thin film over the bottom of the pan; warm the pan to melt the butter, then transfer the sardines to the pan. Heat the mixture until it is warm; then turn the heat to low.

Make the toast and spread it with butter or margarine. Place the toast on the serving plates, and spoon the warm sardines from the pan onto the toast, dividing it into equal portions. Turn off the stove.

Serve immediately.

Welsh Rarebit

(Serves 2 or 3.) This recipe is sometimes referred to as Welsh Rabbit. However an elderly lady once informed me in no uncertain terms that it was Welsh Rarebit. Since the elderly lady was my Welsh grandmother, I have not questioned her pronouncement further. It is a tasty, toasted snack which uses the broiler to melt the toast topping.

Parts List

4 oz (113 gm) of old cheddar cheese
3 tablespoons (45 mL) of milk
1/2 teaspoonful (3 mL) of Worcester sauce
1 tablespoon (15 mL) of butter or margarine
1/3 teaspoonful (2 mL) of dry mustard.
2 slices of bread.

Tools Required

Cheese grater
2 small mixing bowls.
Broiler
Toaster.
Fork

Assembly Instructions

Put the milk, sauce and mustard into one bowl or a cup and blend them together. Grate the cheese into the other bowl. Pour the liquid over the cheese and mix them all together into a gooey mess.

Prepare two slices of toast, butter them and put them on a large plate. Put the oven rack to the top position in the oven, turn the oven to broil, and set the temperature to high. Put a sheet of aluminum foil or a cookie sheet on the shelf in case the cheese runs over. Take the mixture and trowel it roughly onto the pieces of toast using a knife, ensuring that none of the top surface of the toast is visible beyond the mixture. This is necessary to prevent the broiler from burning any exposed areas of the toast.

Place the two pieces of toast on the oven rack under the broiler, with the cheese mixture side up. Let broil for approximately 5 minutes, but watch it. The cheese will melt with the heat and will begin to bubble. Keep watching until the mixture is a nice brown colour.

Turn the broiler off. Remove the rarebit from the oven and serve immediately, but be careful, melted cheese is very hot. Discard the aluminum foil but not the cookie sheet.

Canadian Rarebit

(Serves 2.) I was a teenager living in England at the end of the Second World War. One day my sister and I answered a knock at the door and were given a parcel; closer examination revealed that it was postmarked Buckingham Palace. Our father had died serving with the RAF in Egypt during the war and we anxiously waited for Mother to come home from work to open the parcel. When she did, it was full of canned foods and contained a letter to say that the parcel had originated as a gift from Canada to Her Majesty the Queen to be distributed to war widows and orphans. For us it was a very welcome gift. We ate all the food except for two tins of yellow waxed beans. Since we had never seen waxed beans before, we were at a loss to know how to cook them. We asked around and eventually met a Canadian soldier who suggested we might like to serve them on toast. This recipe followed from that suggestion.

Parts List

> 1 14 oz (398 mL) can cut yellow waxed beans
> 1 5.5 oz (156 mL) can of tomato paste
> 4 oz (113 gm) grated old cheddar cheese
> 1 slice of bread per person
> 1/2 teaspoon (3 mg) oregano
> Butter or margarine.
> Salt and pepper to taste.

Tools Required

> Toaster
> Small cooking pot
> Can opener
> Knife
> Tablespoon
> Serving plates

Assembly Instructions

Melt a little butter in the saucepan using medium heat. Open the can of beans, drain off the fluid and pour the beans into the cooking pot. Open the can of tomato paste and stir the paste in with the beans. Sprinkle with salt and pepper as desired and add the oregano. Warm on the stove on medium heat stirring continuously with the spoon. Turn heat to low.

Make toast using the toast recipe, and spread with butter or margarine. Put the oven rack to the top position in the oven, turn the oven to broil, and set the temperature to high. Put a sheet of aluminum foil or a cookie sheet on the shelf in case the cheese runs over. Take the pot off the stove, and use the spoon to put equal portions of the beans on each piece of toast. Cover the beans with the grated cheese until each piece of toast is completely covered. This is necessary to prevent the broiler from burning any exposed areas of the toast.

Place the pieces of toast on the oven rack under the broiler, with the cheese mixture side up. The cheese will begin to melt with the heat and will combine with the bean mixture. It will then begin to bubble and the top will turn brown. Keep watching and don't let the top burn.

When the cheese has melted and the top is brown, turn the broiler off. Remove the Rarebit from the oven and serve immediately, but be careful, melted cheese is very hot. Discard the aluminum foil.

MRS. MURPHY'S LAW #6

Guests always bring high calorie gifts when you are on a diet.

Soup and Grilled Cheese Sandwich

(Serves 1.) This recipe requires you to do several things at once. Remember how computers time share so that several operations occur simultaneously? Well, you now have to pretend to be a computer and time share your hands. This recipe requires you to warm the soup and grill the sandwich at the same time so that both foods can be served hot together.

Parts List

> 1 10 oz (284 mL) can of soup
> Water if required by recipe
> 2 slices of bread
> Jar of processed cheese spread
> Butter

Tools Required

> Saucepan to hold contents of soup can
> Large spoon for stirring
> Can opener
> Broiler
> Knife

Assembly Instructions

Read the instructions on the can of soup to determine if water should be added. Open the can with the can opener being careful not to cut yourself on the sharp edges of the lid.

Pour the contents into the saucepan, add the water if required and stir to blend with the soup. Put the saucepan on the stove and turn the heat to medium or medium high. Too high a heat may cause the soup to burn on the bottom of the pan.

The soup must be stirred frequently until it comes to the boil. When it boils, turn the heat down until it is just simmering. In between stirs you can prepare the grilled cheese sandwich.

Set the oven rack to the top position under the broiler and put a sheet of aluminum foil on the oven rack. Turn on the broiler to high ready to grill the sandwich. Stir the soup!

Take the two slices of bread and spread processed cheese on one side of each; put the two cheese sides together to make a sandwich. Stir the soup! Now take the sandwich and carefully butter both sides of the bread. You are actually buttering the outside of the sandwich so be careful where you place the buttered side while you butter the other. Stir the soup!

The broiler should be hot by now so place the sandwich under it. You now have to watch the soup and the broiler. This is the time when the telephone rings to offer you a special on something you don't want, or the baby demands that you solve a fundamental biological problem. Stir the soup! Watch the broiler! Attend to the baby's problems! Answer the telephone! The sandwich should turn a golden brown as it grills. As soon as the sandwich is nice and brown remove it, stir the soup, and replace the sandwich to grill the other side.

While the second side is grilling, take the soup, turn off the stove, and pour the soup into the serving bowl. When the second side of the sandwich is brown remove it, turn off the broiler, put the sandwich on a plate, and serve both dishes. If you have time shared well, both items will be hot and neither will be burnt. The baby will also be happy.

SUMMARY

This chapter has concentrated on simple scheduling techniques to enable you to cook with different equipment and serve the food at the correct time, e.g. when it is hot. You have learnt to keep an eye on more than one thing at a time and to cope with distractions at critical times. You are now able to cook food well enough to serve it to unsuspecting customers. Some of the recipes were for two people; I hope you were able to invite someone to share it with you, so you didn't have to eat both servings.

MRS. MURPHY'S LAW #7

The last item prepared will always take twice the stated time to cook.

MRS. MURPHY'S LAW #22

Four year olds never like what is served for supper.

Five year olds never like what is served for supper.

Teenagers don't care what they have for supper as long as there's lots of it.

6. MATURE PRODUCTS
Start thinking about GMP

The previous two chapters covered the basics of cooking and showed how to use the kitchen equipment to produce simple recipes using different ingredients and cooking methods. At this point you know how to cook and can be a little more adventurous. It is time to think about GMP (Good Meal Preparation.) The recipes here are well established and have been passed down from father to son for generations. (Mothers passed them to wives, and the fathers and sons ate them.)

The recipes are straightforward and should give little indigestion if followed carefully. Remember that you are fortunate to have a captive market who can either eat what you put before them, go hungry, or give it to the family pet and take you out to eat for all your hard work. The approximate number of servings are given for each recipe; if it is more than you would normally eat then freeze the leftovers and serve them up as afterburners at a later date. I know that the recipes are suitable for househusbands because my wife refused to let me put them in the book until I had cooked them and my family says that if Dad can cook it, anybody can.

Some of the recipes require vegetables. Vegetables come in many shapes and sizes, and can also be fresh or frozen. Where the recipe calls for vegetables, refer to the chapter on Field Support for assistance on how to prepare and cook them.

One word of advice before you begin. These recipes are a bit more complex than those given before. Read them carefully before you begin to make sure you have all the parts and tools needed and that you know how to schedule the cooking sequence properly.

The recipes have again been divided into groups with two or three recipes per group. The groups are:

Stews
Casseroles
Pasta
Pies
Curries
Meat
Fish
Salads
Sauces

This should provide a good cross-section of typical meals with something to satisfy every taste.

MRS. MURPHY'S LAW #8

If you cook a special meal for house guests, they will have decided to eat out to save you the trouble.

STEWS

Stews are one of the earliest methods of cooking since everything was put into the pot and kept on a low heat until it was cooked. Originally the pot was suspended over an open fire, but today there are more sophisticated pieces of equipment available such as the slow cooker. When cooked in a slow cooker, stew can be prepared and then left to cook while you watch the game on TV, or go and play golf. Stew is also great to return to after the family has been skiing for the day, or it can be cooked the day before, reheated, and put it in a thermos bottle to take to the ski hill. Stews can also be made by simmering them in a large cooking pot, but don't leave them unattended if you are using this method in case they boil dry, and burn. *Remember Mrs. Murphy is always ready to profit by your mistakes.*

If all the stew is not eaten the remainder can be frozen and reheated on the stove or in the microwave, and served as an afterburner at a later date.

Dad's Famous Farmhouse Stew

(Serves 6.) A good stew needs lots of vegetables, and lots of flavouring to mask the taste of the vegetables. I learnt to make stew as a boy when I lived in farming country. It was my job to peel all the vegetables. A stew can be a cheap meal for a lot of people since it uses the cheaper stewing beef and fresh vegetables. This recipe introduces the use of seasonings and wine for flavouring.

Parts List

1 lb (450 gm) of lean stewing beef (cut in small pieces)
1/2 cup (125 mL)flour
6 large carrots
6 parsnips
2 medium onions
1 small rutabaga
3 celery stalks
1 beef bouillon cube or package
1/2 cup (125 mL) beef dripping, or shortening.

Seasonings:
1 bay leaf
1/3 (2 mL) teaspoon of thyme (a dash)
1/3 (2 mL) teaspoon of marjoram
1/3 (2 mL) teaspoon of paprika
1/2 teaspoon (3 mL) of black pepper
1 teaspoon (5 mL) of salt

. . . continued on page 68

1 cup (250 mL) of burgundy (red wine)
Beef gravy thickening as required

Note: Potatoes have not been included because they do not stew well and crumble if cooked too long. Potatoes can be added if desired, but cook them separately 1/2 hour before serving the stew.

Tools Required

Slow cooker or large covered pot (Don't leave a cooking pot on the stove unattended.)
Frying pan
Large cooking spoon
Sharp knife or vegetable peeler
Chopping board
Clean brown paper lunch bag

Assembly Instructions

Check the beef pieces as received from the butcher and if necessary cut them further into bite-size pieces. Pour the flour into the brown lunch bag, add the meat, fold the top of the bag closed (this is very important), and shake the bag like a cocktail shaker. This will coat all the meat with a thin layer of flour. The flour will help thicken the gravy and will add colour and flavour.

Put the dripping in the frying pan, turn the stove to medium high, and melt the dripping. Transfer the pieces of stewing beef from the bag to the pan and put the bag with the remaining flour into the garbage. Fry the beef until the pieces are brown on all sides, turning them frequently. Do not cook them.

Transfer the meat to the slow cooker. Mix up the bouillon according to the instructions, or dissolve it in half a cup of hot water if there are no instructions. Pour the bouillon and the wine over the meat; turn the slow cooker to high heat.

Prepare all the vegetables as described in the Field Support chapter. Slice the carrots and parsnips thinly across and not lengthways, and slice the rutabaga into roughly 1 inch cubes. Slice the celery into 1/2" (10mm) pieces, and cut the onion into quarters. Wash all vegetables thoroughly and put them into the slow cooker.

Put in the bay leaf, and sprinkle the other seasonings on top. Put the lid on the cooker and leave for one hour on high, then turn to low.

The stew can now be left to cook gently for about six hours; it should be stirred a few times to distribute the flavour more evenly. It is cooked when the meat and vegetables are tender.

When you are ready to serve it, add some gravy thickening to the liquid and thicken it following the instructions on the package. Serve the stew hot in bowls with fresh baked bread.

Vegetable Stew

A good flavoured base for a stew can be made from soup bones. Put two pounds (1 kg) of soup bones in a large pan and cover them with water. Put the pan on the stove on high and bring to the boil, then turn the heat down and allow it to simmer until the meat can be removed easily from the bones. Remove all the bones carefully, using a slotted spoon, and then simmer the remaining liquid until half has boiled away. This is referred to as stock. Sometimes cooks exchange this liquid; this is referred to as trading stock or a stock exchange.

Parts List

Soup bone stock
6 large carrots
6 parsnips
2 medium onions
1 small rutabaga
3 celery stalks
1/2 cup (125 mL) dried peas or mixed vegetables
1 beef bouillon cube or package

Seasonings:
1 bay leaf
1/3 teaspoon(2 mL) of thyme (a dash)
1/3 teaspoon (2 mL) of marjoram
1/3 teaspoon (2 mL) of paprika
1/2 teaspoon of black pepper
1 teaspoon (3 mL) of salt
1 cup (250 mL) of burgundy (red wine)
Beef gravy thickening as required

Note: Potatoes have not been included because they do not stew well and crumble if cooked too long. Potatoes can be added if desired, but cook them separately 1/2 hour before serving the stew.

Tools Required

Slow cooker or large covered pot (Don't leave a cooking pot on the stove unattended.)
Large cooking spoon
Slotted kitchen spoon
Sharp knife or vegetable peeler
Chopping board
Small mixing bowl

Assembly Instructions

This stew generates more liquid than the farmhouse stew of the previous recipe, this is compensated for by using the dried vegetables. If these are used they must be prepared the night before. To prepare, put the dried vegetables in the bowl and cover them with water. Leave to soak overnight; the dried vegetables will absorb all the water.

Pour the soup bone stock into the slow cooker, dissolve the bouillon in half a cup of water. Pour the bouillon and the wine into the stock. Add the soaked dried vegetables, and turn the heat to high.

Prepare all the vegetables as described in the Field Support chapter. Slice the carrots and parsnips thinly across and not lengthways, and slice the rutabaga into roughly 1 inch cubes. Slice the celery into 1/2" (10 mm) pieces, and cut the onion into quarters. Wash all vegetables thoroughly and put them into the slow cooker

Put in the bay leaf, and sprinkle the other seasonings on top. Put the lid on the cooker, leave for one hour and then turn to low.

The stew can now be left to simmer gently for about six hours; it should be stirred a few times to distribute the flavour more evenly.

When you are ready to serve it, add some gravy thickening to the liquid and thicken it following the instructions on the package. Serve the stew hot in bowls with fresh baked bread.

MRS. MURPHY'S LAW #9

All laws of physics are repealed for the kitchen.

Hungarian Goulash

(Serves 4.) Hungarian Goulash can be considered a stew or a very thick soup, which is the way it is served in Hungary. It can also be served over a bed of rice as a main dish.

Parts List

1 lb (450 gm) lean stewing beef
2 large Spanish onions
1 green pepper
1 28 oz (796 mL) can tomatoes
1 cup (250 mL) of mushrooms sliced into pieces
2 tablespoons (30 mL) of paprika (that's right)
1 medium clove of garlic
or 1/4 teaspoon (1 mL) of garlic powder
1 teaspoon (5 mL) salt
1/4 teaspoon (1 mL) pepper
2 tablespoons (30 mL) of sour cream
1/2 cup (125 mL) of flour
2 tablespoons (30 mL)of cooking oil or bacon fat

Tools Required

Large frying pan or cooking pot
Can opener
Teaspoon
Tablespoon
Wooden cooking spoon
Clean brown paper lunch bag
Garlic press

Assembly Instructions

Peel and slice the onions into large pieces. Check the beef pieces and if necessary cut them further into bite-size pieces. Pour the flour into the brown lunch bag, add the meat, fold the top of the bag closed (this is very important), and shake the bag like a cocktail shaker. This will coat all the meat with a thin layer of flour. The flour will help thicken the gravy and will add colour and flavour.

Put the dripping in the frying pan or pot, turn the stove to medium high, and melt the dripping. Transfer the pieces of stewing beef from the bag to the pan and put the bag with the remaining flour into the garbage. Fry the beef until the pieces are brown on all sides, turning them frequently. Do not cook them. Add the pieces of onion and sprinkle the paprika over the top. Mix everything together thoroughly.

Open the can of tomatoes, and add the contents to the pan. Press the garlic and add it and the pepper and salt. Bring the mixture to the boil, turn the heat down and allow it to simmer for 2 hours. After one hour of the simmering add the mushrooms. While the mixture is simmering, slice the green pepper following the procedure in the Field Support section, and cut the strips into 3/8 inch squares. Approximately 15 minutes prior to serving add the green pepper; if the pepper is put in too soon it will lose its green colour and texture.

When ready to serve remove from the heat, and stir in the sour cream. Do not boil the sour cream.

Serve as a soup or over a bed of rice.

MRS. MURPHY'S LAW #10

The kitchen garbage can will always be full.

CASSEROLES

Casseroles are prepared in the same dish that they are served in, which reduces the number of dishes to clean after the meal. For this reason they are very popular with gourmet cooks who usually like to cook, but hate to wash up afterwards. In the past this job was usually done by husbands when the teenager was out on a date. However this probably provided the incentive to invent automatic dishwashers so it wasn't a bad thing.

In a casserole the food is prepared and placed directly into the dish. Since the cooked food will be served from the dish, the preparation is done to enhance the appearance at the table. The dish is a special casserole dish which is usually ceramic or oven-proof glassware and can be rectangular or elliptical in shape. It must be deep enough to hold all the juices while the food is cooking, otherwise the overflow will burn on the oven element, and instead of an extra pot you will have an oven to clean.

The Househusband Casserole

(Feeds 4 to 6.) This is a simple casserole to prepare and it tastes great.

Parts List

> 1 lb (450 gm.) ground lean beef
> 1 large Spanish onion
> 1 10 oz (284 mL) can tomato soup
> Jar of processed cheese spread
> Jar of mustard

Tools Required

> Casserole dish
> Knife
> Tablespoon

Assembly Instructions

Turn on the oven to bake at 350°F and set a shelf in the middle.

Make 6 hamburger patties from the ground beef. Lay them in the bottom of the casserole dish, and spread each one with mustard.

Peel the onion and cut it up into 6 round slices; place one piece on each hamburger patty. Put a tablespoonful of cheese spread on each slice of onion. Open the can of tomato soup and pour it over all the patties.

When the oven is up to temperature, put the casserole in the oven and bake for 30 minutes. While the casserole is baking, cook some frozen green vegetables.

Serve when ready. Turn off the oven.

Shepherd's Pie

This recipe is simple to make as long as you have a good source of shepherds and can learn to mash potatoes.

Parts List

1 12 oz (340 gm) can of tinned corned beef
1 cup (250 mL) of frozen peas or corn
6 medium potatoes
1 teaspoon (5 mL) of salt
Small quantity of milk
1/4 cup (60 mL) of ketchup
1/3 teaspoon (2 mL) of Worcester sauce.

Tools Required

Can opener
Casserole dish
Fork
Tablespoon

Assembly Instructions

Put the potatoes on to boil. Follow the recipe for boiled potatoes. While the potatoes are cooking, open the tin of corned beef and put it in a bowl. Mash it up and blend in the ketchup and the Worcester sauce. Add the frozen peas and stir the mix to blend them without mashing them. Spoon the mixture into the bottom of the casserole, and trowel it flat and into all the corners if the dish is square. When the potatoes are cooked, turn on the oven to 350°F.

Drain the potatoes and mash them with a small quantity of milk. Put the mashed potatoes on top of the corned beef mix in the casserole dish, and trowel it flat over the top of the mixture. Make a smooth top, and decorate it with trowelling motifs if you wish. You can also use the tines of the fork to make patterns. The mashed potatoes should cover the entire top.

Place the casserole dish in the oven when it reaches 350°F and bake for 1/2 hour. The mashed potato should have a nice brown crusty tinge when it is cooked.

Remove from the oven and serve immediately after turning off the oven.

Yellow Green Bean Surprise

(Serves 4 to 6.) Some years ago when househusbands were more scarce than they are today, my wife found the cupboard rather bare. With a horde of hungry children to feed she put together what she had, which consisted of yellow and green beans, hamburger, tomato sauce and cheese. The big surprise was that it was an instant success with the kids, so she christened it "Yellow Green Bean Surprise." Here it is!

Parts List

> 1 lb (450 gm) lean ground beef
> 1 14 oz (398 mL) can green beans
> 1 14 oz (398 mL) can yellow beans
> 1 14 oz (398 mL) can of tomato sauce
> 2.5 cups (570 mL) of grated cheddar cheese
> 1 onion

Tools Required

> Casserole dish
> Can opener
> Tablespoon
> Frying pan
> Sharp knife

Assembly Instructions

Turn the oven on to 350°F

Peel and chop the onion. Put a tablespoonful of cooking oil or bacon fat in the frying pan and fry the hamburger and onions until they are brown. Do not cook completely.

Open the cans of beans and put them into the frying pan; add the tomato sauce and a cup of the cheddar cheese. Mix together and put the mixture into the casserole dish. Sprinkle the remaining cheddar cheese over the top of the mixture, but do not stir. Put the dish in the oven and heat until the cheese has melted through the mix, about 30 minutes. When this is done, remove from the oven and serve. Turn off the oven.

PASTA

Pasta is the basis of Italian-style cooking and has the advantage that it is usually one of the less expensive items of food. Pasta itself is a dough which is moulded into many shapes and sizes, processed and put into packets with Mediterranean sounding names like spaghetti, lasagna, linguini, rigatoni, vermicelli and macaroni. Househusbands can purchase the required type from the supermarket where it is in labelled packets. Some pasta is sold with a vegetable green colour which can enhance the appearance of the meal.

Spaghetti

(Serves 6 to 8.) This is a very popular recipe which needs no introduction. Spaghetti is long thin round pasta which comes in a box labelled spaghetti.

Parts List

> 1 lb (450 gm) ground lean beef
> 1 28 oz (796 mL) cans of tomatoes
> 1 5.5 oz (156 mL) can tomato paste
> 1 7.5 oz (213 mL) can tomato sauce
> Sufficient uncooked spaghetti to fit inside a two inch
> diameter circle
> 3 oz (90 mL) Italian seasoning
> 1 tablespoon (15 mL) cooking oil
> 2 medium chopped onions
> Grated parmesan cheese

Tools Required

> Large saucepan
> Spaghetti measure
> Potato masher
> Can opener
> Colander

Assembly Instructions

Pour the cooking oil into the pan and put the pan on the stove; turn it to medium high. Add the hamburger and fry it until it is brown; add the onions.

Drain the tomatoes and add them to the pan. Mash the contents of the pan together with the potato masher. Add the remaining sauces and the seasoning. Turn the heat low so that the sauce is just simmering, and cook for three hours. Alternatively, the sauce can be transferred to a slow cooker and cooked for six hours.

To cook the pasta, half fill a saucepan with water, add a teaspoonful of salt and teaspoon of cooking oil to prevent the pasta from sticking to the pot. Bring to the boil. Add the spaghetti by taking a bunch and putting one end in the boiling water; the immersed end will soften and all the spaghetti will gradually fit in the pot. Allow to boil for ten minutes and then check to see if it's done.

Try the following:

Check for correctly cooked spaghetti.

Remove a piece from the pot using kitchen tongs and, using a soft ball pitch, pitch it at the refrigerator door. If it sticks, its done. Wipe the door off afterwards, and throw away the piece of spaghetti.

Pour the spaghetti into the colander, drain it and put it into a serving dish. Serve onto plates using the tongs, and spoon the sauce over the spaghetti. Sprinkle parmesan cheese over the top.

MRS. MURPHY'S LAW #11

Jam sandwiches always fall face down.

Linguini and Clam Sauce

(Serves 4 to 6.) If you like pasta recipes, this is a simple one to try; it was passed on to me by some college students. Linguini is the long thin flat pasta; if you can get the green (verdi) version it adds some colour contrast to the dish.

Parts List

2 10 oz (568 mL) cans of clams
2 tablespoons (30 mL) of butter
1 packet (255 mL) of linguini
1 tablespoon (30 mL)of lemon sauce
8 oz (450 gm) Philadelphia cream cheese
1 medium clove of garlic
or 1/4 teaspoon (1 mL) of garlic powder
1 teaspoon (5 mL) of salt
1 teaspoon (5 mL) of cooking oil

Tools Required

Frying pan
Saucepan
Tablespoon
Garlic press
Colander

Assembly Instructions

To cook the pasta, half fill a saucepan with water, add the salt and the teaspoon of cooking oil to prevent the pasta from sticking to the pot. Turn the heat to high and bring the water to the boil. Add the linguini, turn the heat to medium and boil for ten minutes.

Put the butter in the frying pan, put the pan on the stove, and turn to medium high. When the butter has melted, add the clams, the lemon juice, and the cream cheese. Stir the mixture until the cheese has melted. Press the clove of garlic and add it to the mixture or sprinkle with garlic powder to taste.

Turn the heat to low to keep it warm.

Remove the linguini from the heat when it is cooked, turn the stove element off, pour the linguini into the colander and allow to drain, then put it in a serving bowl. Remove the clams from the stove, turn that element off also, and pour the clam sauce over the linguini. Serve immediately while warm.

Lasagna

(Serves 6.) Lasagna is baked as a casserole. This recipe will fit in an 8" x 12" casserole dish. Lasagna is the wide flat pasta with wavy edges.

Parts List

> 1 lb (450 gm) lean ground beef
> 14 oz (398 mL) can tomato sauce
> 1 Packet of lasagna noodle (You will need enough noodles to completely cover the casserole dish twice.)
> 1.5 oz (43 gm) packet of spaghetti sauce mix
> 1 lb (450 gm) tub of cottage cheese
> 1 lb (450 gm) package mozzarella cheese slices (not processed cheese)
> Cooking oil or cooking spray
> Parmesan cheese

Tools Required

> Frying pan
> Can opener
> Wooden kitchen spoon
> Tablespoon
> Saucepan
> Casserole dish
> Colander

Assembly Instructions

To cook the pasta, half fill a saucepan with water, add a teaspoonful of salt and a teaspoon of cooking oil to prevent the pasta from sticking to the pot. Turn the heat to high and bring the water to the boil. Add the lasagna, turn the heat to medium and boil for ten minutes or until the pasta is soft. Do not overcook. Pour into the colander, drain the water and allow to cool. Turn off the element.

To make the sauce, put two tablespoons of cooking oil in the frying pan and turn the heat to medium high; when the oil is warm add the ground beef and brown it. Add the package of spaghetti sauce mix and the contents of the tin of tomatoes. Cook for ten minutes, then turn the heat off.

Turn the oven on to 350°F.

Coat the casserole dish with a thin layer of cooking oil to prevent the sauce from sticking to it. Spread two tablespoons of the cooked sauce over the bottom of the pan, then cover the sauce with a layer of noodles.

Spread a second layer of the cooked sauce over the top of the noodles, then cover this with 4 large tablespoons (60 mL) of cottage cheese. Cover the layer of cottage cheese with a layer of the slices of mozzarella cheese, covering the pan completely, then add a further layer of noodles. Put four more tablespoons of cottage cheese on top and cover with a final layer of mozzarella cheese. Shake parmesan cheese over the top.

Put in the oven and cook for 45 minutes. When cooked, remove from the oven and let sit for 10 minutes for the cheese to firm up, allowing the lasagna to cut easily.

Cut into squares for serving, and serve with a Caesar salad and crusty bread rolls.

MRS. MURPHY'S LAW #12

If the cake is mixed perfectly, there will be a power failure while it is cooking.

PIES

Pies usually conjure up a picture of a pastry shell filled with either savoury meat or fruit. However, pies do not have to be associated with pastry as illustrated by the Shepherd's Pie casserole. Many of the traditional types of pie were made and sold by the pie man who sold both large and small individual pies. His trade has become a lucrative fast food business in Australia where pie shops serving individual hot pies can be found on many street corners. In North America the pie man has been replaced by the frozen pie which is available in considerable variety in supermarkets. Cooking instructions on a typical frozen meat pie are:

Preheat oven to 375°F. Heat for 35 minutes and serve.

With the availability of this type of pie, the househusband need not consider baking the traditional pies, and need only concern himself with pies which are best made and cooked in the kitchen or are not yet available in prefabricated form.

The following two recipes are for this type of pie.

Cheese and Ham Pie

(Serves 4.) There was a rumour circulating a few years ago that real men would not eat quiche. In case you subscribe to that philosophy and would be embarrassed to be seen buying a frozen quiche, I have changed the name to Cheese and Ham Pie. It is, however, cooked in a quiche dish rather than a regular pie dish, because otherwise you would have to clean up a very messy oven. A quiche dish is deeper than the normal pie dish and the pie is less likely to boil over.

There is no real problem for real men making pastry; buy a frozen pie shell and from there on it's quite straightforward.

Parts List

1 frozen uncooked pie shell
1 6.5 oz (184 gm) tin of flakes of ham
1/4 lb (130 gm) Gruyere cheese
1/4 cup (60 mL) frozen chopped onion
3 eggs
1 5.6 oz (160 mL) can of evaporated milk
1/2 cup (125 mL) of fresh milk
1/8 teaspoonful (0.5 mL) of cayenne pepper

Tools Required

1 deep pie dish (Use a quiche dish if you have one)
Egg beater
Measuring cups
Mixing bowl
Can opener

Assembly Instructions

Allow the pie shell to defrost, then transfer it carefully to the pie dish. Arrange it to cover the entire dish bottom and sides. You will find defrosted pastry behaves rather like dry plasticine or putty.

Turn on the oven and set it to 400°F; put the oven shelf in the middle. Open the tin of flakes of ham, and grate the cheese. Spread the ham and grated cheese together with the onion over the bottom of the pie shell, rather like a bed of gravel for a path.

Break the eggs one at a time and put the contents into the mixing bowl. Beat them, and then add the evaporated milk and the fresh milk. Blend together; this mixture is referred to as custard. Pour the custard into the pie shell. If the pie shell is going to overflow, stop pouring.

When the oven is at 400°F, put the quiche, sorry . . . pie, into the oven and bake for 20 minutes. Without taking the pie out of the oven, turn the oven down to 300°F and bake it for a further 20 minutes. The pie is cooked when the custard is firm and not liquid. The pie is ruined when the custard is black.

Remove from the oven using oven mitts to handle. Serve hot or cold with a salad.

MRS. MURPHY'S LAW #13

Never trust a fat cook. Nobody will eat their food and they have to eat it all themselves.

Rice Cheese and Tomato Pie

(Serves 2.) This pie recipe is unique because it uses rice in place of pastry.

Parts List

2 oz (57 gm) long grain rice
4 oz (130 gm) old cheddar cheese
2 fresh tomatoes
1 onion
Packet of breadcrumbs (seasoned if available)
1 tablespoon (15 mL) of butter

Tools Required

Cooking pot for the rice
Cheese grater
Several small bowls for cheese, etc.
Kettle
Pie dish

Assembly Instructions

Cook the rice following the instructions on the package. Turn the oven on to 375°F and put the shelf in the middle. Boil some water in the kettle.

While the rice is cooking, cut up the onion into small pieces and grate the cheese into a bowl. Use the water from the kettle to simplify peeling the tomatoes following the technique given in the Field Support section. When they are peeled, slice the tomatoes in the transverse plane. Use the butter to put a thin layer of fat over the inside of the pie dish.

When the rice is cooked, spread it in a layer over the bottom of the pie dish, then spread half the grated cheese over the top of the rice. Spread the onion bits over the cheese and then put the sliced tomatoes on top so that they cover the contents of the dish. Spread the rest of the cheese over the top of the pie, then cover the cheese with a thin layer of breadcrumbs.

When the oven is hot, put the pie in the oven and bake for 30 minutes. (It is useful to put some aluminum foil on the oven shelf in case the cheese boils over.) While cooking, the cheese will melt into the rice and tomatoes, and the breadcrumbs will become a top crust.

When done, remove from the oven using oven mitts. Serve with a salad.

CURRIES

Curries can be made with most cooked meats, the usual ones being chicken, turkey, beef and lamb. Curry is a hot seasoning which can be purchased at the supermarket in three grades, mild, medium and WTH (Wow! That's Hot). There is a great temptation to drink lots of fluid if the curry is WTH, but according to some experts this should not be done because it spreads the 'hot' oils in the curry over a bigger area. They recommend eating simple boiled rice or bread to absorb the 'hot' oils.

Curried Turkey

(Serves 4 to 6.) The recipe given here is great for using up leftover turkey from Thanksgiving, Christmas or any other time there is a surplus of cold turkey.

Parts List

2 to 3 cups (500 - 750 mL) of cooked turkey, cut into small cubes.
4 tablespoons (60 mL) of butter or margarine
3 teaspoons (15 mL) of curry powder.
1/2 cup (125 mL) of chopped onion
3 tablespoons (45 mL) of all purpose flour
2 packages or cubes of chicken bouillon
(Use beef bouillon for beef or lamb)
1/4 cup (60 mL) of chopped unsalted cashews
2 teaspoons (10 mL) of lemon juice
2 Granny Smith apples
1/2 cup (125 mL) of raisins
1/2 teaspoon (3 mL) salt
1/3 teaspoon (2 mL) pepper
2/3 cup (150 mL) of long grain rice

Tools Required

Medium or large frying pan
Covered pot for the rice.
Wooden kitchen spoon
Kettle
Measuring cups
Small mixing bowl
Sharp knife

Assembly Instructions

Peel and chop into small pieces enough onion to equal half a cup. Put water in the kettle and bring it to the boil. Put the bouillon into a small mixing bowl and add 2 cups (500 mL) of boiling water. Stir until dissolved, then put it to one side to use later.

Read the instructions on the package for cooking the rice, or use the instructions for your microwave oven. While the rice is cooking, put the frying pan on the stove and turn the heat to medium high. Melt the butter and tilt the pan around so that it covers the bottom. Add the curry powder and stir until mixed. Add the onion and cook until tender.

Add the flour, salt and pepper and stir well (you do this so that the mixture is well blended), then add the bouillon which you made. Heat until the mixture is boiling, then turn the heat down and let it simmer for a further 2 minutes.

Peel the apples as described in the Field Support chapter, cut them into wedge sections, and remove the seed core. Then cut the wedges into bite-size pieces. Add the apples to the pan, then put in the nuts, raisins, lemon juice and turkey. Allow to simmer for another 5 minutes, or until the rice is cooked.

Serve with the rice, putting the rice on the plate and spooning the curry over the rice.

MRS. MURPHY'S LAW #14

Never trust a thin cook. They are not prepared to eat their own food.

Curry in a Bag

(Serves 1 starving student or 2 adults.) In case you are puzzled by the name of this recipe, it was passed on to a university student by his mother who told him to use the curry in a bag which you buy from the health food store. Now you know where to buy the curry. If you don't have any curry in a bag, use your regular brand.

Parts List

1 6.5 oz (184 gm) can of solid cut tuna
1 Granny Smith apple
2 level tablespoons (30 mL) of flour
1/2 cup (125 mL) of milk
2 teaspoons (10 mL) of vinegar
1 packet of chicken bouillon
1 tablespoon (15 mL) of lemon juice
2 level teaspoons (30 mL) of curry (from the bag)
2/3 cup (150 mL) of long grain rice

Tools Required

Frying pan
Pot for cooking rice
Can opener
Wooden kitchen spoon
Sharp knife
Tablespoon
teaspoon
2 cups
Set of measuring cups
Kettle

Assembly Instructions

Read the instructions on the package for cooking the rice, or use the instructions for your microwave oven, and put the rice on to cook. While the rice is cooking, put the kettle on to boil some water. While it is heating, put the flour in a cup and add cold water to make a flour and water paste. The paste can be mixed the same way that you would mix plaster patching compound, but it should be slightly runnier. Add the curry (from the bag) and half a cup of milk. Stir to remove any lumps.

When the water boils, empty the contents of the bouillon package into a cup. Add half a cup of boiling water and stir until the powder dissolves.

Peel the apples as described in the Field Support chapter, cut them into wedge sections and remove the seed core. Then cut the wedges into small (less than bite-size) pieces.

Open the tin of tuna and pour the juice into the frying pan. Add the vinegar. Put the pan on the stove, turn the heat to high and sauté the apple in the juice for about five minutes. Sauté refers to the technique of frying while stirring and moving everything around quickly with the wooden spoon.

Turn the heat to medium, add the flour and curry mixture and half a cup of water. Stir, then add the bouillon mixture and the lemon juice. Continue to stir until the contents are hot. Remove from the stove and put into a serving bowl. Turn the burner off.

Serve over the rice.

MRS. MURPHY'S LAW #15

There will always be one less plate setting available than the number of guests for dinner.

MEAT

Although some of the previous recipes have contained meat, the meat has been combined with other ingredients to create the dish. With the following recipes, the meat is the basic dish which is normally served up with some form of vegetable.

Pork Chops and Mushroom Sauce

(Serves 4.)

Parts List

4 lean pork chops
1 10 oz (284 mL) can of mushroom soup
1 beef bouillon cube
2 tablespoonfuls (30 mL) of cooking oil

Tools Required

Frying pan
Can opener
Kitchen tongs
Wooden kitchen spoon
Cup
Tongs or fork
Kettle

Assembly Instructions

Put the kettle on to boil some water. Pour the cooking oil into the frying pan and put the pan on the stove with medium high heat. Put the pork chops in the pan, and let them cook until they are nicely brown on one side. Turn them over with the tongs or a fork and brown the other side. When the water boils, put the bouillon in a cup, add boiling water, and stir to mix.

When the pork chops are browned on both sides, open the can of soup and pour the soup and the bouillon over the chops. Turn the heat down so that the mixture is simmering and leave for fifteen minutes.

Transfer to a serving dish, and serve with cooked frozen vegetables of your choice.

Honey Chicken

(Serves 4.) I have no idea why this is called honey chicken unless the result is honey coloured. My daughter, whose recipe it is, calls it that and she doesn't know either.

Parts List

4 pieces of boneless chicken
1/2 cup (125 mL) of corn syrup
1/3 cup (130 mL) of barbecue sauce
2 tablespoons (30 mL) of cooking oil

Tools Required

Frying pan with a lid
Measuring cups
Wooden kitchen spoon
Small mixing bowl
Kitchen tongs or fork

Assembly Instructions

Put the frying pan on the stove, pour in the cooking oil and turn the heat to high. When the oil is hot, put in the chicken and fry it until it is lightly brown on one side. Use the tongs or a fork to turn the pieces over and brown the other side.

Mix the sauce and corn syrup together in the bowl and pour it over the browned chicken. Turn the heat to low, put the lid on the frying pan and cook for 20 minutes.

Serve with your favourite cooked vegetables.

MRS. MURPHY'S LAW #16

Plastic wrap clings well. Usually to itself.

Mixed Grill

This is a popular restaurant meal in the U.K. It consists of several different meats fried together. The selection of meats is chosen for the taste variety, and you can vary it to suit yourself. Only use baby beef liver in this recipe because other liver tends to be tough and strong tasting. The quantities are given per person. Serve it with vegetables of your choice.

Parts List

1 lamb chop
1 1/4 lb (112 gm) steak filet
1 Bavarian or English sausage
2 oz (56 gm) baby beef liver
3 or 4 slices of bacon
1 piece of beef kidney
1 egg
2 tablespoons (30 mL) of cooking oil

Tools Required

Frying pan
Egg lifter
Sharp knife
Cutting board
Large plate

Assembly Instructions

Make sure the oven is empty, put a large plate on the shelf and turn the heat to 200°F. Cut the meat from the kidney and cut it into small pieces. Put the cooking oil into the frying pan, put it on the stove and turn the heat to medium high. When the oil is hot put in all the meat, distributing it around the pan. The lamb chop, the steak fillet and the bacon can be cooked as you prefer, anything from just past raw (rare) to black (well done). When these are cooked as you wish, transfer them from the pan to the plate in the warm oven. The other meats must be cooked thoroughly by turning them frequently until they are well browned on all sides. If in doubt go around one more time. When they are cooked, transfer them also to the oven.

Break the egg and put the contents into the frying pan. There should be sufficient cooking fat in the pan from the meats, but if not add two more tablespoons of cooking oil. Fry the egg and either turn it over or spoon hot fat over the top until the yolk clouds over. Remove the egg with the egg lifter and transfer it to the plate in the oven. Serve while hot.

Horse Meat Deluxe

(Serves 1.) During a business trip to Paris which lasted several months, I ate frequently at a particular restaurant. One night the special on the menu was "Steak Haché à Cheval", which I translated as minced horse meat. I didn't order it, but it intrigued me and I saw it on the menu several times over the next few weeks. Finally my curiosity got the better of me and one night I ordered it. What I got was a regular beef hamburger with a fried egg on top! I subsequently discovered that the correct title was "Steak Haché, œuf à cheval," i.e. minced steak with an egg riding horseback. So here is the recipe for the horse meat special!

Parts List

> 1/4 lb (113 gm) ground steak
> 1 egg
> 2 tablespoons (30 mL) of cooking oil

Tools Required

> Frying pan
> Egg lifter
> Tablespoon

Assembly Instructions

Make the ground steak into a single hamburger patty. Break the egg and put the contents into a cup. Put the cooking oil in the frying pan, put the pan on the stove and turn the heat to medium high. Put the hamburger in the pan, brown one side, turn it over and brown the other.

Tilt the pan slightly so that the hot fat is on one side and pour the egg into the fat. Tilting the pan ensures that the egg white remains close to the egg. The egg white will be clear when the egg is put in, but will turn white as it cooks. When most of the white has turned, turn the egg over with the egg lifter if you prefer your eggs 'over'. If you prefer them 'sunny', use the spoon to drip hot fat over the top of the egg until a film begins to form over the egg yolk. The egg is now cooked. Turn the hamburger over and place the egg on top. Leave a short while longer, about a minute, then remove the hamburger and the egg together and serve.

If you wish you can cook some frozen vegetables in the microwave at the same time as the 'horse meat' is cooking.

Ginger Beef and Broccoli

(Serves 2.) It is better to cook this dish in a wok, but you can use a frying pan if you don't have a wok. A wok is a hemispherical-shaped frying pan used for oriental cooking. The shape allows all the cooking fluids to drain into the bottom so that less fat is required. Also because the heat can only be applied to the bottom, it is possible to move food that is cooking too quickly to the cooler outer edges while cooking the rest. The following assembly instructions are for cooking with a wok.

Parts List

1/2 lb sirloin steak
1/2 lb (225 gm) fresh mushrooms **or** 1 10 oz can
1 head fresh broccoli
1 medium onion
2 teaspoons (10 mL) of ginger
3 teaspoons (15 mL) of olive oil
3 tablespoons (45 mL) of soya sauce
2/3 cup (150 mL) long grain rice

Tools Required

Wok or frying pan
Wooden kitchen spoon
Can opener if using canned mushrooms
Sharp knife
Cutting board

Assembly Instructions

Slice the beef into thin flat slices, about 3/16 " (5 mm) thick. The beef will slice easier if it is slightly frozen first. Peel and cut up the onion into small pieces. Prepare the broccoli by cutting off the flowerets from the main and side stalks to make small (1.5" or 40 mm) long pieces. Wash thoroughly under clean water, and put aside to drain. Wash the mushrooms, cut off the bottom of the stem and cut them in halves or quarters.

Read the instructions on the package for cooking the rice, or use the instructions for your microwave oven, and start cooking the rice. While the rice is cooking, put the olive oil in the wok, put it on the burner and turn the heat to high. When the oil is hot add the onions and brown them, turning frequently with the kitchen spoon. Move them out to the cooler side and put the beef in the hot centre. Stir it continually to brown it. Sprinkle the ginger over the beef, and add the mushrooms while still stirring.

When the mushrooms are warm, part the mixture in the middle to make a space and put the broccoli in the space. Warm the broccoli, stirring it continuously. Add the soya sauce and stir everything together to combine all the flavours. With all the stirring you can understand why these dishes are referred to as 'Stir Fry'.

Serve with the rice.

Dad's Beef Pot Roast

(Serves 4.) Pot roast, as its name implies, is a roast cooked in a pot. The meat is really stewed in its own juices, rather than roasted, and for this reason you can use a cheaper cut of beef. The butcher at the supermarket can advise you about the cuts suitable for a good pot roast.

Parts List

3 or 4 pound (1.5 - 2 Kg) beef pot roast
6 large carrots
6 parsnips
2 medium onions
3 celery stalks
6 medium potatoes
1 beef bouillon cube or package
Beef gravy thickening as required.
3 tablespoons (45 mL) cooking oil
1 cup (250 mL) of flour

Seasonings:
1 bay leaf
1/3 teaspoon (2 mL) of thyme (a dash)
1/3 teaspoon (2 mL) of marjoram
1/3 teaspoon (2 mL) of paprika
1/2 teaspoon (3 mL) of black pepper
1 teaspoon (5 mL) of salt
1/2 cup (125 mL) of burgundy (red wine)

Tools Required

Frying pan
Slow cooker
Pot for the potatoes
Sharp knife
Cutting board
Kettle
Cup
Barbecue tools
Colander

Assembly Instructions

Put some water in the kettle and put it on to boil. Put the bouillon into the cup, and when the water boils make a cup of bouillon. While the water is heating, cut any external fat from the pot roast. Caution: if the roast is tied with string be careful not to cut the string. Sprinkle the flour onto the cutting board, and roll the meat in it so that it is coated in flour. Put the cooking oil in the frying pan, put the pan on the stove, and turn the heat to high. Put the roast in the pan and brown it on all sides. using the larger barbecue tools to handle the meat. Transfer the meat to the slow cooker, and turn off the stove. Add the wine and the bouillon, and the bay leaf. Sprinkle the thyme, marjoram, paprika, pepper and salt over the meat. Turn the heat to high and put the lid on.

Dust the flour off the cutting board and wash it. Peel and slice the carrots, parsnips and onions, following the procedures given in the Field Support chapter. Clean and cut the celery into 1/2" or 12 mm pieces. Add the vegetables to the slow cooker and leave them cooking for five hours. After five hours, peel the potatoes and cook them following the instructions in the Field Support chapter. When they are cooked, turn the heat off.

Turn the slow cooker off and transfer the pot roast to a serving plate. Spoon the vegetables from the cooker and arrange them around the roast on the dish. Pour the potatoes into the colander and drain the water off, then arrange the potatoes around the meat.

Pour the juice from the slow cooker into a small pan, put it on the stove and heat it. Add sufficient gravy thickening to make a thick gravy and pour it into a serving jug.

Carve the pot roast at the dinner table with a sharp knife or an electric carver, and serve the vegetables from the platter onto individual plates using a serving spoon.

MRS. MURPHY'S LAW #17

Sugar bowls and butter dishes always hide during meal preparation.

Oven Roasting

Beef, pork, lamb, chicken and turkey are all suitable for oven roasting. The meat is cooked in the oven, and then carved into slices after cooking. Traditionally beef is served with Yorkshire pudding, pork is served with apple sauce, lamb is served with mint sauce, and turkey is served with cranberry sauce. Chicken can be served with honey. Roasting a turkey for a big meal such as Thanksgiving or Christmas is the final exercise in this book and is the official FAT (Family Acceptance Test). During FAT you can demonstrate your new-found kitchen skills to unsuspecting relatives, and if your sister-in-law doesn't complain you can consider that you have passed. The following recipe is for a red meat roast, and it gives you a chance to practise the technique of roasting before you undertake the FAT.

Roast Beef and Yorkshire Pudding

(Serves 4.) This Yorkshire pudding recipe comes directly from my wife who is from Yorkshire. The pudding is made as a batter which is then cooked in a hot oven. When mixed correctly the batter rises rather like blowing up an air mattress, but if it's not done properly, it resembles a leaky air mattress. My daughter spent many hours trying to make Yorkshire pudding rise without any success. One day her younger sister was giving her a hard time, whereupon Lynda suggested that the younger sister try. Always ready for a challenge, Michelle did, and of course it rose immediately.

The beef is roasted in an open roasting pan in a moderately hot oven, and the fat which drains into the pan from the meat is used to roast the potatoes at the same time. The butcher at the supermarket can advise you on the cuts of beef suitable for oven roasting; unfortunately these cuts tend to be the more expensive ones, so this is unlikely to be an everyday recipe.

Parts List

3 or 4 pound (1.5 - 2 Kg) prime beef roast
2 cups (500 mL) frozen carrots
2 cups (500 mL) frozen brussels sprouts
6 medium potatoes
Packet of gravy thickener
2 tablespoons (30 mL) beef dripping or cooking fat
8 heaped tablespoons (120 mL) of flour
2 eggs
Milk
Salt to taste

Tools Required

Roasting pan
Saucepans for vegetables
Small and medium mixing bowls
Sharp knife
Fork
Colander
Kitchen tongs

Assembly Instructions

Turn the oven on to 350°F and set the shelf to one of the lower positions. Check the roast for fat; if it has very little, coat the outside with the beef dripping as if you were buttering bread. This will prevent the outside from burning. Put the roast in the oven. After 1/2 hour turn the heat down to 325°F. Using the hotter temperature initially seals the outside of the meat.

As soon as the roast is in the oven, peel the potatoes and put them in a pan to boil, adding a teaspoonful of salt. Boil for 15 minutes, then transfer the contents to the colander and drain. Open the oven and remove the roast. Place the potatoes around the outside using the tongs and roll them in the hot drippings and beef juices. Replace the roasting pan in the oven. Leave to cook until the total time for the roast in the oven is between 2 1/4 (rare) and 2 3/4 hours (well done). Remove from the oven and allow to stand. The meat will carve better if it is cooler.

At this point the vegetables should either be ready for the microwave, or ready to go into pots of boiling water. Start the vegetables, then make the Yorkshire pudding.

Yorkshire Pudding

Set the oven to 450°F. Put the flour into the mixing bowl. Break the eggs, make a hole in the middle of the flour as for mixing cement or plaster, and put the whole eggs into the hole. Mix the eggs and flour to make a smooth paste. Add the milk, a small quantity at a time, until the mixture has the consistency of thick cream, beating well to ensure proper blending.

Put the two tablespoons of beef drippings or bacon fat in a shallow cooking tray or pan, and place in the oven. Make sure the fat covers the entire bottom of the pan. When the fat is really hot, blue smoke will begin to rise. When it reaches this temperature, slide out the oven rack with the tray on it (using oven mitts) and carefully pour the pudding batter into the dish. Be careful, everything will be very hot. Push the shelf back in, close the oven door and cook for ten minutes. The pudding should have risen by that time, and will be a light brown colour. Don't worry if it doesn't rise, it will still taste good, but not as good. Remove the pudding from the oven and turn the oven off.

While the Yorkshire pudding is cooking, transfer the meat and potatoes to a serving platter. Pour the juices from the bottom of the pan into a small sauce pan to make some gravy, put it on the stove, and turn the stove to high. If there is insufficient liquid, add some water and bring to the boil. Add some gravy thickener as specified on the packet, remove from the stove, turn the stove off, and pour the gravy into a jug.

At this point you have a roast of beef, Yorkshire pudding which should be cut up into 2" (50 mm) squares to serve, and the vegetables which should be put into dishes to serve. Carve the beef into thin slices, cutting across the grain of the meat as for a piece of 2 x 4, and put it on the individual plates.

FISH

Fish which is not freshly caught develops a strong unpleasant flavour, and many people associate this flavour with fish. This is the reason why more people appear to enjoy fish if they live in a coastal region than if they live several hundred miles inland. Inland, frozen fish can be better than so-called fresh fish. The taste of fish is also governed by the cooking time. If overcooked it gets tough, and if undercooked the taste is strong. Fish is correctly cooked when the outside is still moist and the individual sections of flesh separate easily with a knife. The following two recipes are for frozen fish.

Sole and Parsley Sauce

Parts List

4 frozen sole fillets
2 oz (113 gm) butter
16 oz (450 mL) milk
1/4 cup (60 mL) white wine
1/4 cup (60 mL) parsley bits

Tools Required

Saucepan
Microwave dish to hold the fish
Spoon
Fork
Measuring cups
Egg lifter

Assembly Instructions

Put the sole fillets in the dish and place in the microwave oven. Turn the oven on to high for 6 minutes.

This recipe uses the basic white sauce mix listed under sauces. Mix the sauce following the basic recipe. When the sauce thickens, remove the pan from the heat and stir in the wine and the parsley.

Put the sole on a serving dish and pour the sauce over the top. Serve with cooked frozen vegetables.

Bajun Salmon Poached in Wine

(Serves 4.) Bajun salmon is a contradiction because salmon does not come from Barbados. However Barbados produces a delicious chopped seasoning which tastes great with fish, and includes onions, shallots, thyme, marjoram, sweet basil, sweet pepper, hot pepper, garlic, powdered clove, black pepper, salt and vinegar. With all that how could anything be tasteless. If you cannot get the true Bajun seasoning at a food speciality store, you could always try making your own in small quantities.

Parts List

4 salmon steaks
2 tablespoons (30 mL) of butter
2 teaspoons (10 mL) of Bajun chopped seasoning
1 cup (250 mL) of white wine
1 teaspoon (5 mL) of lemon juice

Tools Required

Frying pan with a lid
Egg lifter
Sharp knife

Assembly Instructions

Make shallow cuts across the surface of one side of the steaks; this will allow the seasoning to penetrate into the fish. Put the white wine into a cup, add the lemon juice and stir.

Put the frying pan onto the stove and turn to high, put in the butter and melt it until it froths. Put the salmon steaks into the pan, cut side first, and lightly brown both sides. This will leave the cut side upwards when both sides are brown. Put half a teaspoon of the seasoning on each steak, and spread it over the surface.

Pour the wine mixture into the frying pan, but do not pour over the fish. Allow the wine to boil until half has boiled away, then cover the pan and turn the heat to medium. Cook for 5 minutes. Check that the steaks are done by ensuring that the flesh segments separate easily.

Serve with cooked vegetables in winter, or with a Caesar salad in summer.

SAUCES

Sauces refer to creamy like liquids which are served hot and poured over food prior to serving to keep it warm, improve its appearance and add flavour. This recipe describes a basic white sauce which can then be modified, for example by adding parsley bits and serving with fish, or adding cheese and serving over cauliflower or broccoli.

White Sauce

Parts List

> 2 tablespoons (30 mL) of butter or margarine
> 2 tablespoons (30 mL) of enriched flour
> 1 cup (250 mL) of milk
> Salt and pepper to taste.

Tools Required

> Small saucepan
> Tablespoon

Assembly Instructions

It is essential to use a low heat for this, otherwise the sauce will be burnt or lumpy.

Melt the butter or margarine in the saucepan on low or medium low heat. When the fat is liquid, add the flour gradually, stirring all the time. If the heat is too high, remove the pan from the stove while the element is cooling, and keep stirring.

Gradually add the milk. Keep stirring as the liquid heats until it reaches boiling point, when the mixture will thicken.

When the mixture has thickened, remove it from the heat, turn the stove off, and pour the sauce into a small jug for serving.

Cheese Sauce

Parts List

2 tablespoons (30 mL) of butter or margarine
2 tablespoons (30 mL) of enriched flour
1 cup (250 mL) of milk
1 cup (250 mL) of grated cheddar cheese
Salt and pepper to taste

Tools Required

Small saucepan
Tablespoon

Assembly Instructions

It is essential to use a low heat for this, otherwise the sauce will be burnt, or lumpy.

Melt the butter or margarine in the saucepan on low or medium low heat. When the fat is liquid, add the flour gradually, stirring all the time. If the heat is too high, remove the pan from the stove while the element is cooling and keep stirring.

Gradually add the milk, and then add the cheese. Keep stirring as the liquid heats. As it reaches boiling point, the cheese will have melted, and the mixture will thicken.

When the mixture has thickened, remove it from the heat, turn the stove off, and pour the sauce into a small jug for serving.

SALADS

Salad is the name given to dishes of mixed cold food; frequently one of the items is lettuce. Salads can be a complete meal in themselves, especially when cold turkey, chicken, ham. shrimps, cheese or similar food is used as a base. When served this way the salad is referred to by the name of the base i.e. turkey salad, ham salad, shrimp salad. Salad made with mixed fruits is referred to as a fruit salad; however, don't expect to find chuck wagons in a chuck wagon salad, or chefs in a chef's salad. It pays to be a bit cautious when ordering salad: I was in a restaurant in the south of France and ordered the tomato salad which was listed on the menu. I got a plate of sliced tomatoes with an olive oil dressing!

Green salads are ones in which lettuce, spinach or cabbage is used as the main ingredient. Usually a thick sauce is poured over the final product and mixed in with everything; this is referred to as dressing the salad, and the sauce is called salad dressing. The process of mixing the dressing into the salad is known as tossing the salad. That's a bit more mumbo jumbo for you to learn.

Salads can be very nutritional and are ideal for the diet-conscious person who frequently chooses salads because of their low calorie content and high nutritional value, and then soaks everything in high-calorie dressing.

One point of caution with salads. Since they are not cooked, bacteria which would normally be destroyed by heat will still be there. It is, therefore, very important to wash all the raw food carefully.

Simple Salad

This simple salad is a basic lettuce salad which can be served with many meals. Try it with soup to have soup and salad.

Parts List

1 lettuce
1 tomato
1 cucumber or zucchini
6 radishes (in season)
1 egg
1 bottle of salad dressing of your choice

. . . continued on page 104

Tools Required

Bowl large enough to hold the salad
Saucepan to boil the egg
Sharp knife
Chopping board
Tablespoon
Salad serving spoons

Assembly Instructions

Put sufficient water in the pot to cover the egg and put the saucepan on the stove. Turn the stove on high and bring the water to a brisk boil. Turn the heat to medium, and put the egg in the boiling water. Leave the egg in boiling water for ten minutes to become hard-boiled. Remove the egg from the pan using the spoon, and turn off the stove. Run the hot egg under the cold tap to make it easier to remove the shell. Crack the shell lightly and peel the shell off.

While the egg is boiling you have ten minutes to prepare as much of the other food as you can. Peel back two or three inches of the cucumber, and slice the peeled section into thin slices. If you are using a zucchini do not peel it, wash the skin, cut off two to three inches off the end and slice this into thin slices. Put the slices on a plate.

Wash the radishes, cut the top and bottom ends off, and slice into thin decorative slices. Put the radish slices with the cucumber or zucchini. Wash the tomato and cut it into about eight sections, then cut these sections in half. Put these sections on a separate plate.

Take the lettuce and remove any outer brown leaves. Wash the remainder in running water and make sure it is clean. Tear the lettuce into bite-size pieces. Dry them by patting with a clean towel, and place the pieces in the bowl. Add the cucumber or zucchini and the radishes.

Pour salad dressing on the contents of the bowl; then take the two salad serving spoons and 'toss the salad'.

This does not imply that you should throw it in the garbage. Put the spoons into the bottom of the bowl and carefully lift the contents upwards in successive motions so that you mix the salad dressing and the contents together.

Take the egg and cut it into thin slices. Now, remembering your lessons in salesmanship, you can start making the salad look attractive by placing the slices of egg and tomato alternatively round the edge of the bowl. If there is any tomato left over, arrange the remainder in the middle.

Caution: If you toss the egg and tomato with the rest of the salad, the egg will break up and the tomato juice will dilute the salad dressing and it becomes "Yuk" salad.

Caesar Salad

Produce this one and people will begin to be impressed. "Hey, Dad is getting good. He can make a Caesar Salad."

Parts List

1 romaine lettuce
8 slices streaky bacon
Box of Caesar salad croutons
Bottle of Caesar salad dressing

Tools Required

Frying pan
Salad bowl
Salad serving spoon

Assembly Instructions

Place the bacon in the frying pan, put the pan on the stove and turn the heat to high. When the bacon starts to sizzle, turn the heat down so that the fat which will come out of the bacon doesn't splatter all over you. Cook the bacon until it is crisp, but not burnt, and remove it from the pan. Take the pan off the stove and turn the heat off.

Take the outer leaves off the romaine lettuce and discard them. Take the remainder of the leaves off, and wash them thoroughly. After washing them, dry them carefully with a clean towel. Tear the leaves up into bite sized pieces and place them in the salad bowl.

Allow the bacon to cool, then crumble it up into small crumbs, and sprinkle it over the lettuce, then sprinkle a cup of Caesar salad croutons over the mixture.

Pour 3/4 of a cup of salad dressing over the salad, and 'toss the salad.' If you have forgotten how, refer to the recipe for a simple salad.

Creamy Potato Salad

A potato salad is great with other salads and also in the summer with barbecued meats. It is very easy to make now that you know how to boil eggs and potatoes.

Parts List

6 medium sized potatoes
4 eggs
1 Jar of mayonnaise
1 tablespoon (15 mL) of white vinegar
2 tablespoons (30 mL) of chopped onion (Frozen chopped onion is ideal.)
1 cup (250 mL) of finely chopped celery
1 teaspoonful (5 mL) of salt
Salt and pepper to taste.
Paprika
Several thin slices of peeled cucumber

Tools Required

2 saucepans
2 mixing bowls
2 tablespoons
1 measuring cup

Assembly Instructions

Peel the potatoes, wash them thoroughly, and put them in one of the saucepans. Cover with water, add the salt, put the lid on and place the pan on the stove. Turn on to high. When the water is boiling turn down to medium, so that the water remains boiling, and boil until the potatoes are soft cooked (approximately 20 minutes).

While the potatoes are boiling, put enough water in the other pan to cover the eggs. Put the lid on the pan, put the pan on the stove, turn the stove to high and bring the water to a brisk boil. Add the eggs, turn the heat to medium, and boil for ten minutes. Take the pan off the stove, turn the heat off, and cool the eggs in cold water.

Remove the potatoes from the stove, drain them and put them in a bowl. Add three tablespoons of mayonnaise and one tablespoon of white vinegar while the potatoes are still warm and mash them lightly. They should not be mashed to a creamy mixture. The mayonnaise should be partly absorbed into the potato surface.

Peel the eggs and place them in another bowl. Chop them up using a spoon, add salt and pepper as required, add chopped onion and cup of celery, and blend everything together.

Put everything into one bowl, add a tablespoon of mayonnaise and mix together.

Put in the refrigerator until ready to serve. When ready to serve, put slices of cucumber on top, and sprinkle paprika over for colour.

MRS. MURPHY'S LAW #19

If the meal is on time, the diners will be late.

Corollary: If the diners are on time, something unforseen will delay the meal.

AFTERBURNERS

Afterburners are great because you have an opportunity to burn the same dish twice, once when cooking and once when reheating.

Reheating

It is frequently necessary to reheat food because of the late arrival of family members due to 'circumstances beyond their control?' If you have a microwave, put the food in a covered dish, or on a plate covered with microwave-proof plastic wrap, and heat it on medium until hot. For oven reheating set the oven to 200°F and put the food in a covered dish or put another plate upside down on top. Heat until warm.

Bubble and Squeak

Bubble and Squeak is an excellent afterburner dish, prepared from left over vegetables. Put a small quantity of beef dripping or cooking oil in a frying pan, and put the leftover vegetables in the pan. Fry the vegetables, mixing them all together, until the outside has turned golden brown. Serve immediately before it becomes leftover Bubble and Squeak.

Hot Meat Sandwich

Frequently, cold meat is left over from a roast. Beef, turkey, pork or lamb together with the leftover gravy in the jug can be served as an afterburner by putting slices of meat between two slices of bread on a plate and pouring reheated gravy over the top to make a hot meal. Serve with cooked vegetables for a complete meal.

SUMMARY

This chapter has given you good practice at making meals from established recipes, and you should now have the courage to look at the recipe books again. If you have successfully cooked the recipes in this chapter together with some vegetables from the Field Support chapter, you should now be able to use a regular recipe book. We have not yet tackled any desserts, so you can now move on and learn how to program the software.

7. FIELD SUPPORT
Where all the dirty work is done

It is not the intention of this chapter to give a detailed description of all vegetables, but to give an overview of the more common ones so that you know how to prepare and cook them.

Vegetables are basic for meal preparation; they provide many essential vitamins and minerals, and 'they are good for you', remember? You say you are a meat-and-potatoes man? OK, but did you know that potatoes are vegetables? Many vegetables can be eaten raw, in salads for example. In general, vegetables should be prepared just before use if served raw, or immediately before cooking. Some root vegetables can be prepared one or two hours ahead of time but they must be kept under water in a pot until they can be cooked. Vegetables should always be fresh or still frozen, and should always be served immediately after cooking since some of the vitamins deteriorate with time when they are kept warm.

FROZEN VEGETABLES

Frozen vegetables are the easiest way for a beginner to start cooking, and some vegetables, such as peas and green beans, are much quicker to prepare when frozen. Anyone who has had to shuck peas (remove them from the shell) or slice green beans will agree. When frozen, peas have been removed from the pod and beans have been sliced. Frozen vegetables are already prepared and can be cooked directly from the package. There are two methods which can be used: the conventional method using boiling water in a saucepan, and the microwave method. First check the package to see if cooking instructions are provided. If not proceed as follows.

Conventional Cooking

Parts List

> 1 cup of frozen vegetables
> Salt to taste (1 teaspoon)

Tools Required

> Saucepan to hold vegetables
> Slotted spoon or colander
> Water as required

Assembly Instructions

Do not thaw the vegetables.

Fill the saucepan half full with water and add the salt. Put the lid on the pot, put the pot on the stove and turn the heat on to high. Bring the water to a brisk boil, remove the cover and add the frozen vegetables. The cold vegetables will cool the water. Bring it to a boil again and reduce the setting to medium. Ensure the water does not stop boiling.

Cook gently for 5 to 7 minutes. Use the spoon to remove a small portion of veretables from the pot and check to see if they are tender. When tender, take the pot off the heat, turn off the stove and remove the lid. Pour the contents into a colander to separate the vegetables from the liquids and put the vegetables into a serving dish. Alternatively use the slotted spoon to remove the vegetables from the pot.

Microwave Cooking

Parts List

1 package of frozen vegetables
Salt to taste (1 teaspoon)

Tools Required

Microwave oven
Covered microwave dish for vegetables
Tablespoon

Assembly Instructions

Do not thaw the vegetables.

Put the required amount of vegetables in the microwave dish and put the cover on. Set the microwave to high and cook for 7 to 9 minutes until vegetables are tender. After 3 minutes, interrupt the oven, open the door, remove the cover and stir the vegetables. Replace the cover and continue cooking for the remainder of the time. When the oven turns off, let the dish remain in the oven for a further two minutes.

Remove the dish from the oven and put it on the table. Careful! Put a mat underneath so that you don't damage the table finish.

GREEN VEGETABLES

It is a surprising thing for kitchen jargon, but green vegetables are usually green. Many cooking terms are misleading, but in this case greens are green and the terms greens and green have nothing to do with golf.

Common green vegetables are:

- Lettuce
- Peas
- Runner or French Beans
- Cabbage
- Broccoli
- Cauliflower
- Brussels Sprouts

Lettuce is eaten raw in salads. The uses of lettuce are covered in the salad section in the mature products chapter.

As mentioned previously, peas and beans are probably best cooked frozen, so shucking peas, i.e. removing them from the pod, and slicing beans have not been included.

Cabbage

Cabbage can be eaten raw or cooked; raw cabbage is used for coleslaw.

Parts List

1 fresh small green cabbage
1 teaspoon of salt
Water as required

Tools Required

Saucepan large enough to hold the cabbage
Sharp knife
Tablespoon
Colander

Assembly Instructions

Prepare the cabbage just before cooking. Strip off any brown outer leaves and throw them away or, if you have one, put them in the composter. Cut the remainder into 6 to 8 segments and throw away any damaged or brown bits. Wash thoroughly. Fill about a quarter of the saucepan with water, and add the cabbage and salt if desired. Put the lid on the saucepan and the saucepan on the stove. Turn the heat to high and bring the water to a brisk boil. As soon as the water boils turn the heat down so that the water is just boiling.

Check after 10 minutes. The cabbage will be tender, i.e. soft when cooked. Watch to see that the pot does not boil dry.

When cooked, remove the pot from the stove, and turn the stove off. Place the colander in the sink and pour the contents of the saucepan into it. When the water has drained away transfer the cabbage to a serving dish. Serve immediately while hot.

Brussels Sprouts

These look like very small cabbages and are served cooked.

Parts List

> 1 lb (450 gm) fresh brussels sprouts
> 1 teaspoonful (5 mL) of salt

Tools Required

> Saucepan large enough to hold the sprouts
> Sharp knife
> Tablespoon
> Colander

Assembly Instructions

Trim off any brown or discoloured outer leaves, and wash thoroughly. Sprouts are usually cooked whole, but they can be cut in half if you suspect that they are not sound in the middle.

Wash thoroughly. Fill about a quarter of the saucepan with water, and add the sprouts and the salt if desired. Put the lid on the saucepan and the saucepan on the stove. Turn the heat to high and bring the water to a brisk boil. As soon as the water boils turn the heat down so that the water is just boiling.

Check after 10 minutes. The sprouts will be tender if cooked. If not cooked, replace the lid and check every three minutes. Watch to see that the pot does not boil dry.

When cooked, remove the pot from the stove, turn the stove off. Place the colander in the sink and pour the contents of the saucepan into it. When the water has drained away transfer the sprouts to a serving dish. Serve immediately while hot. If you wish to add a gourmet touch, put a small piece of butter on top of the sprouts so that it melts over them.

Cauliflower

Cauliflower looks like a cabbage with a white 'flower' in the centre. The edible part is the white flower which can be cooked whole or separated into little flowerets. This recipe describes the cooking of the flowerets since these are quicker and do not require cutting to serve.

Parts List

> 1 small cauliflower
> 1 teaspoon (5 mL) of salt
> Ingredients for sauce

Tools Required

> Saucepan large enough to hold the flowerets
> Sharp knife
> Tablespoon
> Colander

Assembly Instructions

Strip off all the outer green leaves, leaving only the white flower. With the knife cut the branches of the flower to make small (about 1.5" or 40 mm long) flowerets.

Wash thoroughly. Fill about a quarter of the saucepan with water and add the flowerets and the salt if desired. Put the lid on the saucepan and the saucepan on the stove. Turn the heat to high and bring the water to a brisk boil. As soon as the water boils turn the heat down so that the water is just boiling.

Check after 10 minutes. The flowerets will be tender if cooked. If not cooked, replace the lid and check every three minutes. Watch to see that the pot does not boil dry.

When the cauliflower is cooked, remove the pot from the stove and turn the stove off. Place the colander in the sink and pour the contents of the saucepan into it. When the water has drained away transfer the flowerets to a serving dish. Serve immediately while hot. Cauliflower can be made more tasty by making a cheese sauce to spread over the top. A suitable sauce is given in the Mature Products chapter.

Broccoli

Broccoli resembles a small green tree with branches. The main stalk can be rather tough and stringy, but the flowerets on the ends of the 'branches' are quite tasty, especially when served with a sauce.

Parts List

> 1 small broccoli
> 1 teaspoon (5mL) of salt
> Ingredients for sauce

Tools Required

> Saucepan large enough to hold the flowerets
> Sharp knife
> Tablespoon
> Colander

Assembly Instructions

Cut off the flowerets from the main and side stalks to make small (about 1.5" or 40 mm long) flowerets.

Wash thoroughly. Fill about a quarter of the saucepan with water, and add the flowerets and the salt if desired. Put the lid on the saucepan and the saucepan on the stove. Turn the heat to high and bring the water to a brisk boil. As soon as the water boils turn the heat down so that the water is just boiling.

Check after 10 minutes. The flowerets will be tender if cooked. If not cooked, replace the lid and check every three minutes. Watch to see that the pot does not boil dry.

When cooked, remove the pot from the stove and turn the stove off. Place the colander in the sink and pour the contents of the saucepan into it. When the water has drained away transfer the flowerets to a serving dish. Serve immediately while hot. Broccoli can be made more tasty by making a cheese sauce to spread over the top. The cheese sauce from the Mature Products chapter can be used for this.

ROOT VEGETABLES

If you are a purist you may argue that some of the vegetables described in this section are not 'roots'. I won't argue with you, but as far as I am concerned if it flies through the air it could be a baseball, a football or an aeroplane, and if it comes from underground it's a root.

Root vegetables have a firm interior and are covered with a protective skin which usually has to be peeled off with a vegetable peeler or a sharp knife. The skin can be left on if you are baking potatoes in the oven, or if you have small early crop new potatoes or carrots. In peeling, the object is to remove the skin and leave as much of the vegetable being peeled as possible.

Take the vegetable in one hand and carefully remove a thin layer of the skin in one stroke of the knife. Repeat this until all the skin has been removed. Since the skin is a protective coating, most vegetables go brown soon after peeling, and it is advisable to peel items immediately prior to use and not before. To reduce the browning effect immerse the item in water after peeling.

Boiled Potatoes

The humble potato has developed a reputation among the diet conscious which it does not deserve. People avoid it because it is 'high in calories.' Remember, 'a calorie is a calorie is a calorie', and the average boiled potato has about 100. Compare this with a cup of cottage cheese, a real favourite with the diet conscious, which has around 200 calories. Simple boiled potatoes are not very tasty and the taste is often varied by adding a sauce or by mashing them with milk and butter which definitely increases the calorie content. If they are mashed with milk and butter, potato calories go up to 195, but with milk they only go up to 135. Hardly justification for its bad reputation. They can be boiled as follows.

Parts List

> 4 medium potatoes
> 1 teaspoon (5mL) of salt

Tools Required

> Saucepan large enough to hold the potatoes
> Sharp knife or potato peeler
> Fork
> Colander

Assembly Instructions

Peel each potato. Allow the peelings to drop onto an open sheet of newspaper; they will be much easier to clean up afterwards. (Potato peelings make good compost.) Cut the peeled potatoes into halves or quarters, depending on the size of the individual potato. Wash thoroughly by putting them in the colander and running cold tap water over them.

Put the potatoes in the saucepan, and add sufficient water to cover them. Add the salt if desired. Put the lid on the saucepan and the saucepan on the stove. Turn the heat to high and bring the water to a brisk boil. As soon as the water boils, turn the heat down so that the water is just boiling.

Check after 20 minutes. Try to put the fork into one of the potatoes; if it can be pushed through easily, the potatoes are cooked. If you cannot push the fork all the way through, replace the lid and check every five minutes. Watch to see that the pot does not boil dry.

When cooked, remove the pot from the stove, and turn the stove off. Place the colander in the sink and pour the contents of the saucepan into it. When the water has drained away transfer the potatoes to a bowl. At this point the potatoes are cooked, and they can be served immediately while hot, or they can be treated as required for a specific recipe.

Mashed Potatoes

One of the more popular ways of serving potatoes is to mash them.

Parts List

> 4 medium potatoes
> 1 teaspoon (5mL) of salt
> Small jug of milk
> Butter if desired

Tools Required

> Saucepan large enough to hold the potatoes
> Sharp knife or potato peeler
> Tablespoon
> Fork
> Colander
> Potato masher or fork
> Bowl for mashing

Assembly Instructions

Boil the potatoes; when they are cooked drain them in the colander, and put them in the bowl. Mash them by hand using a potato masher or fork, and break them up until they have a wet powdery consistency. A mixer can be used for this if you have one. Pour in a small drop of milk, and continue mashing. Add milk until the mix looks like patching plaster. It should cling to the tool but be quite smooth with no lumps.

A creamier mixture can be obtained if some butter or 1/2 cup (125 mL) of sour cream is added together with the milk, but this will increase the calories so the choice is yours. Pepper and salt can also be added for taste.

Serve immediately while warm; there is nothing worse than cold mashed potatoes.

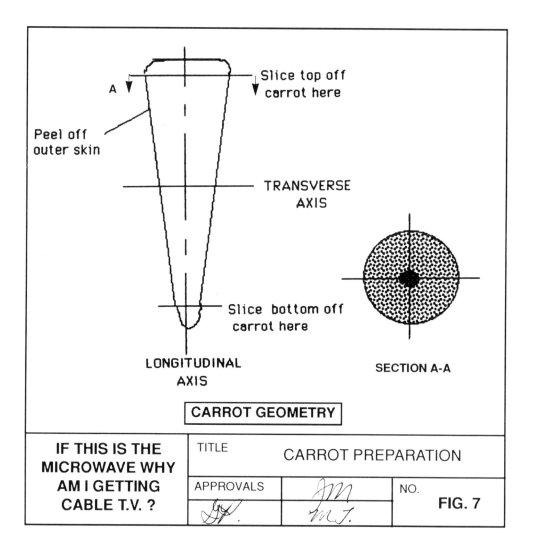

CARROT GEOMETRY

IF THIS IS THE MICROWAVE WHY AM I GETTING CABLE T.V. ?	TITLE	CARROT PREPARATION	
	APPROVALS		NO. FIG. 7

Carrots

Frozen carrots are very good with many meals, but some meals such as stews are better with fresh carrots. Carrots are reputed to improve night vision, but this is based on the fact that the code name for night radar during the second world war was 'carrots'. Obviously 'carrots' did help night fighters see in the dark.

Fresh carrots are cooked as follows:

Parts List

> 1 lb (450 gm) carrots
> 1 teaspoon (5 mL) of salt

Tools Required

> Saucepan large enough to hold the carrots
> Sharp knife or vegetable peeler
> Fork
> Colander

Assembly Instructions

Refer to Figure 7. The carrot is approximately conical in shape, with a longitudinal and a transverse axis. Cut the top and bottom ends off the carrots and peel each one as indicated in the figure; if the skin is thin it may be possible to scrape the skin off with the knife edge. Allow the peelings or scrapings to drop onto an open sheet of newspaper, and they will be much easier to clean up afterwards and put on the compost. After peeling, slice the carrots either along the transverse axis (as for a cross cut on a 2x4) or lengthways along the longitudinal axis (as when using a rip saw). This will give you either thin circles of carrot or thin strips; the choice is yours. If the circles are large in diameter, cut into halves or quarters. Wash thoroughly by putting pieces into the colander and running cold tap water over them.

Put the carrots in the saucepan, and add sufficient water to cover them. Add the salt if desired. Put the lid on the saucepan and the saucepan on the stove. Turn the heat to high and bring the water to a brisk boil. As soon as the water boils, turn the heat down so that the water is just boiling.

Check after 15 minutes. Try to put the fork into one of the carrots, if it can be pushed through easily, the carrots are cooked. If you cannot push the fork all the way through, replace the lid and check every five minutes. Watch to see that the pot does not boil dry.

When cooked, remove the pot from the stove, and turn the stove off. Place the colander in the sink and pour the contents of the saucepan into it.

When the water has drained away transfer the carrots to a bowl. At this point the carrots are cooked, and they can be served immediately while hot. For added taste, sprinkle brown sugar on top and allow a piece of butter to melt over them.

Parsnips

Parsnips are a root vegetable rather like a white carrot. I have always been told that they are much sweeter to taste if they are dug up after the first frost, but I have never verified this. Preparation and cooking are the same as for carrots; refer to Figure 7 for details. No! they don't help you see in the dark either.

Rutabaga

Rutabagas are also referred to as Swedish turnips or simply as Swedes. They vary in diameter from about 4 to 8 inches and are a very tough vegetable to cut. When cooked they are quite soft and can be mashed if desired.

Parts List

> 1 small rutabaga
> 1 teaspoon (5mL) of salt

Tools Required

> Saucepan large enough to hold the rutabaga
> when cut up
> Vegetable peeler
> Large strong sharp knife
> Fork
> Colander

Assembly Instructions

Rutabagas create a special problem because of their size and hardness. They are best cut into smaller pieces using a sharp knife, after which these pieces can be peeled. It is very difficult to cut them in halves and quarters. After peeling, the slices can be washed and then cut into bite-size pieces.

Put the pieces in the saucepan, and add sufficient water to cover them. Add the salt if desired. Put the lid on the saucepan and the saucepan on the stove. Turn the heat to high and bring the water to a brisk boil. As soon as the water boils, turn the heat down so that the water is just boiling.

Check after 30 minutes. Try to put the fork into one of the pieces; if it can be pushed through easily, the pieces are cooked. If you cannot push the fork all the way through, replace the lid and check every five minutes. Watch to see that the pot does not boil dry.

When cooked, remove the pot from the stove, and turn the stove off. Place the colander in the sink and pour the contents of the saucepan into it. When the water has drained away transfer the pieces to a bowl. At this point the pieces are cooked, and they can be served immediately while hot. If preferred they can be mashed with butter, as for potatoes. A little sprinkle of nutmeg adds a spicy flavour.

SQUASH

Some vegetables grow above the ground, some below the ground, and some grow on the ground. For the want of a better name, I have labelled all the vegetables that grow on the ground 'Squash'.

This type of vegetable usually has a high water content and the vegetable can be up to 18 inches in length with a diameter of 6 to 9 inches. Some are rounder like the pumpkin.

Acorn Squash

Parts List

> 1 small acorn squash
> 1 teaspoon (5 mL) of salt

Tools Required

> Saucepan large enough to hold the squash after it has been cut into cubes.
> Sharp knife or vegetable peeler
> Fork
> Colander

Assembly Instructions

Cut the squash in two halves, lengthways. In the middle there will be a stringy core which is full of seeds. Remove all of this core and the seeds and throw away. Peel each half of the squash. If you allow the peelings to drop onto an open sheet of newspaper, they will be much easier to clean up afterwards. Cut the squash into approximately 1 inch cubes. Wash thoroughly by putting the pieces in the colander and running cold tap water over them.

Put the squash pieces in the saucepan, and add sufficient water to cover them. Add the salt if desired. Put the lid on the saucepan and the saucepan on the stove. Turn the heat to high and bring the water to a brisk boil. As soon as the water boils turn the heat down so that the water is just boiling.

Check after 15 minutes. Try to put the fork into one of the pieces; if it can be pushed through easily, the squash is cooked. If you cannot push the fork all the way through, replace the lid and check every three minutes. Watch to see that the pot does not boil dry.

When cooked, remove the pot from the stove, and turn the stove off. Place the colander in the sink and pour the contents of the saucepan into it. When the water has drained away transfer the squash to a bowl. At this point it is cooked and can be served immediately while hot, or it can be treated as required for a specific recipe.

Zucchini

Zucchini is a very popular squash which comes in many sizes. The large versions can be treated as for the acorn squash. The smaller ones are very tasty if thin slices are cooked in a small frying pan. Proceed as follows:

Parts List

> 1 or two small zucchinis
> Small quantity of butter or cooking oil
> Grated Parmesan cheese

Tools Required

> Frying pan or skillet
> Fork

Assembly Instructions

Wash the zucchini, but do not peel. Cut the zucchini into thin slices, discarding the ends where the centre area is not clearly defined.

Put the frying pan on the stove, and turn the heat to high. Melt enough butter in the pan to cover the bottom, or use sufficient cooking oil to achieve the same thing. When the pan is hot, turn the heat to medium and place the pieces of zucchini on the bottom. Sprinkle on pepper and salt. Cook for approximately 5 minutes, turning the slices over frequently with the fork until they brown slightly on both sides. Sprinkle with parmesan cheese and cook for another minute. The pieces should be soft. Remove from the pan and serve hot as a vegetable or as a snack.

ONIONS

Onions have a rather special place in cooking; many people have shed tears trying to prepare them. If you find you have the same problem, prepare them under water.

There are many types of onion including regular, Spanish, shallots, leeks, spring onions and garlic. With the exception of leeks, they are not often cooked as a vegetable on their own. In the majority of cases, onions are used for flavouring and are called for as part of a separate recipe.

Regular Onions

Regular and Spanish onions, and shallots, are prepared as follows:

Preparation

> Cut off the top of the onion where the stalk was
> Cut off the bottom where the roots grew

Insert a sharp knife point under the outer dry skin and holding the skin between the knife blade and a thumb, pull the skin off. The skin should pull off easily, and if you are lucky and careful you can probably pull off the entire layer. Repeat this process until the pure white onion is exposed with no coloured skin. Wipe your eyes.

If the recipe calls for the onion to be cut, place the onion on a chopping board, and cut it into slices like the carrots, or the recipe may call for it to be cut in quarters or crosswise in rings.

After cutting up onions always wash chopping boards and knives carefully because onions have a very strong flavour which can linger for a long time.

Spring Onions

Spring onions are small baby onions which are very popular for use in salads. They have long, soft, green stems with a small white bulb at the end. All the onion is eaten. Prepare as follows:

Use a sharp knife and cut off the bottom portion of the white section where the roots come out. Leave as much of the white as possible. Cut off any discoloured green stems and about an inch off the end. Then cut the onion into 1" lengths or serve uncut after washing. When eaten whole the onion can be dipped in salt for added flavour.

Leeks

Leeks look rather like large spring onions with flat leaves. They have a distinctive, mild onion flavour, and can be served as a vegetable with a sauce or used in stews and soup. Prepare as follows:

Wash the leeks, cut off the root portion as for spring onions, and cut the greens about 2" above the white portion. Place in a saucepan and fill the pan 1/4 full with water. Put the lid on the saucepan. Add a teaspoon of salt, put the pan on the stove, turn the stove to high, and boil the water. When the water is boiling turn the heat down and boil for 15 to 20 minutes. Drain in a colander and serve as a vegetable with a cheese sauce.

Garlic

Garlic is used as a flavouring and is very strong. Garlic is a bulb in an onion type housing, but on closer inspection the bulb consists of individual segments called cloves. To prepare a garlic clove, a special garlic press is required. The clove is inserted in the press and squeezed so that the clove is crushed into tiny pieces. These pieces are then put into the recipe. Sometimes the recipe will call for the glove to be rubbed over the inside of the serving bowl. Garlic is strong enough that this will impart sufficient flavour to the food. To do this, cut the tip off the clove and rub the open end all over the surface. Discard the clove when finished.

MRS. MURPHY'S LAW #20

Coles Law. Pickled Cabbage.

PREPARING SALAD VEGETABLES

Many raw vegetables can be used in a salad, or the vegetables can be arranged attractively around a large plate, with a dip in a dish in the middle. The basic vegetable for a salad is the lettuce and the preparation for this is given in the salad section. Other vegetables which can be used are:

> Broccoli head
> Cauliflower
> Small cherry tomatoes
> Regular tomatoes
> Apples
> Mushrooms
> Zucchini
> Carrots
> Celery stalks
> Cucumber

Tools Required

> Sharp knife
> Cutting board

Prepare the individual vegetables as follows:

Broccoli   Cut the flowerets off the top of the stalks, wash carefully and put in a plastic bag until ready to use.

Cauliflower   Cut into sections and cut the flowerets off. Wash carefully and put in a plastic bag until ready to use.

Cherry Tomatoes Remove the stalk from the top of the tomato. Wash carefully.

Regular Tomatoes Remove the stalk from the top of the tomato and wash carefully. Refer to Figure 8. The tomato and apple have approximately the same shape. Cut the tomato into eight wedges around the vertical axis as shown in the figure. Tomatoes can also be sliced thinly parallel to the transverse axis.

Note: If a recipe calls for the tomato to be peeled, this can be done very easily if the tomato is soaked for a minute in boiling water first. Insert the point of the knife under the skin and the skin will peel off by pulling, rather like peeling an onion.

Apples

Apples are peeled and are then sliced into wedges as shown in Figure 8. Apples have seeds in the centre with a tough membrane between the seeds and the edible flesh. Cut the seed portion out after cutting into wedges. Apples must be served immediately to prevent them from discolouring.

Mushrooms

Wash carefully. Cut off the bottom of the stems and then slice the mushrooms in half. Put in plastic bag.

Zucchini

Do not peel. Cut about an inch off each end and cut the remainder into thin slices. Put in plastic bag.

Carrots

Scrape or peel the carrots and cut them into thin strips so that one end can be put in the dip before eating. Put in a plastic bag.

Celery

Clean the celery, and scrape off any blemishes; use the inner parts of the celery bunch. Cut the celery stalks into three inch long sticks, and fill the inside trough with cheese spread.

Cucumber

Cut the end off, then slice in thin slices like the zucchini. The cucumber can be peeled if the skin is a bit tough. Afterwards it can be soaked in vinegar if desired.

Green Peppers

Green peppers have an outer shell which is crisp and sweet to taste. The inside is hollow with many hot pepper seeds and if you don't wish to suffer from WTH these must be discarded. Slice the pepper into 16 segments through the stalk scar at the top; each segment will be about 3/8" wide. Carefully remove ALL of the white seeds. When serving with a vegetable platter and dip, leave the pepper as strips, but if serving in a salad, cut the strips into pieces about 1/2" long.

Dip

Select a pre-packaged dip for use with sour cream, and make up according to the directions. Another tasty dip can be made by blending sour cream and a powdered onion soup mix. (If you can't find it look for it in aisle 4 between the soap powder and the sugar.)

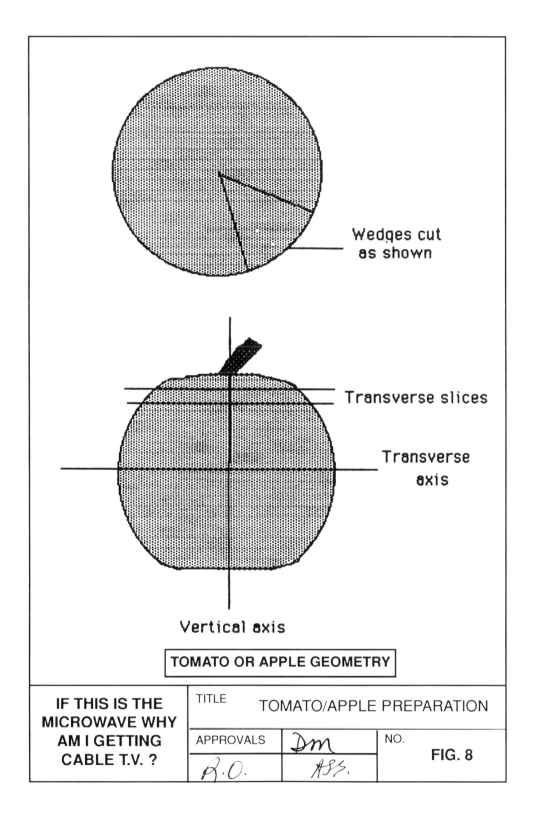

Wedges cut
as shown

Transverse slices

Transverse
axis

Vertical axis

TOMATO OR APPLE GEOMETRY

IF THIS IS THE MICROWAVE WHY AM I GETTING CABLE T.V. ?	TITLE	TOMATO/APPLE PREPARATION	
	APPROVALS	𝒟m	NO.
	R.O.	ASS.	FIG. 8

RICE

Rice is a very versatile vegetable which is served with many oriental dishes and is a good substitute for potatoes if preferred. It can be served by itself, or mixed with small pieces of meat, fish or shrimp as in Chicken Fried Rice. It can also be mixed with butter, milk, or sugar and jam to make a dessert.

It is cooked by frying, or by boiling in water until all the water has been absorbed by the rice, and the rice is soft. The final result should be rice which is soft and doesn't cling together in a lumpy mass.

When boiled it can be cooked either by boiling in a pot on the stove, or by boiling in a covered dish in the microwave. Usually the package gives instructions for each method, but if you threw the package out before you read the directions try the following. The recipe is sufficient for four people.

Parts List

1 cup (250 mL) of long grain rice
2 cups (500 mL) of water
2 teaspoons (10 mL) of butter
1 teaspoon (5 mL) of salt

Tools Required

Saucepan
Kitchen spoon
2 quart (2 litre) covered casserole for microwave method

Assembly Instructions

Stove Top Method   Put all ingredients into the saucepan, put the lid on the pan, put the pan on the stove and turn the burner to high. When the water boils turn the heat to medium low and allow it to boil for 20 minutes, but do not let it boil over. The object is to keep it boiling so the water will be absorbed into the rice. Remove the cover and check that the water has been absorbed; if not, replace the cover and cook for five additional minutes. Do not let the pan boil dry. Remove the pan from the stove and let it stand covered for five minutes.

Microwave Method   Put all the ingredients into the casserole and cover it. Place casserole in the microwave oven and turn the oven on to high to boil the water, approximately four minutes. When the water boils, turn the heat to medium low and cook for a further 20 minutes. Check that the water has been absorbed. Continue cooking if necessary, then let it stand for five minutes before serving.

SUMMARY

This chapter concentrated on the preparation of vegetable dishes using either frozen or fresh products. Preparation of green and root vegetables, squash and rice was described. These dishes are not normally meals in themselves, but are used to complete the main dishes of a meal.

MRS. MURPHY'S LAW #21

Clean floors attract raw eggs.

MRS. MURPHY'S LAW #18

The telephone will ring as your sauce, which needs constant stirring, comes to the boil.

The telephone will ring again as you take your souffle out of the oven.

The telephone will ring again as the milk boils over.

If the telephone rings while you are cooking it will be somebody selling something you have no need for.

8. SOFTWARE
Very User Friendly

To the uninitiated, software is an obscure science which produces some rather awesome results. The same can be said about desserts; they can look very exotic, but in point of fact they are usually something mundane covered in whipped cream with a cherry on top. With this kind of software the only hard disk you will find is a cookie; however, if the dessert becomes stale it becomes hardware.

ICE CREAM

Ice cream is probably the simplest dessert to make look attractive with a little imagination. The following suggestions should start you on your way.

Sundaes

Sundaes are a typical example of something ordinary made to look exotic because they consist of ice cream, flavouring and whipped cream. It is all a question of whether you serve up a dish of ice cream or, with a little extra effort, a sundae. The flavourings are just a matter of personal choice. Experiment and make up your own combinations.

Parts List

> 1 carton of ice cream
> Fresh, frozen or tinned fruit
> Ice cream topping
> 1 can of whipped cream

Tools Required

Ice cream scoop or strong spoon
Shallow dish
Can opener for tinned fruit
Sharp knife for fresh fruit

Assembly Instructions

First prepare the fruit; either defrost it, open it, or peel and cut it up. Scoop a liberal portion of ice cream into individual bowls, and put two tablespoonsful of fruit over the top. Pour the ice cream topping over the top so that it runs over the ice cream and mixes with the fruit. Cover the top of the ice cream with the whipped cream, and put a maraschino cherry on top. It is advisable to spray a little bit of the whipped cream into a saucer before you direct it at the sundae so that you learn how to use the spray; otherwise you may blast the cream and the fruit all over the kitchen. (Remember clean up spills immediately.)

Ice cream must be prepared immediately prior to eating. You can, however, put the ice cream into the bowls prior to the meal, and then place the bowls in the freezer until you are ready.

Parfait

The ice cream parfait is as easy to make as the sundae, but looks even better. It is best served in a fluted glass which is a glass shaped like an inverted cone with a flat base. This will display the different layers of the parfait clearly. If you don't have a fluted glass, use a large brandy glass. I would not recommend using a beer stein, it will not have the desired effect.

Parts List

1 carton of ice cream
1 oz. (30 mL) liqueur, or flavoured cordial
1 can of whipped cream

Tools Required

Parfait or brandy glasses
Spoons which will reach to the bottom of the glass
Ice cream scoop or strong spoon

Assembly Instructions

Put a liberal scoop of ice cream into the glass, and pour the liqueur over the ice cream. Put whipped cream on top and add a cherry, or a chocolate wafer on top. Serve immediately.

Raspberry Delight

(Serves 6 to 8.) I came across a similar dessert in a restaurant when I was in Paris. You can often make quite easy desserts by noting the ingredients and then experimenting to suit your taste. This is how this dessert came into being.

Parts List

1 carton of raspberry sherbet (ice cream)
1 packet of frozen raspberries
1 oz (30 mL) of brandy per serving
(Don't use your best extra Napoleon for this, use a less expensive brand.)

Tools Required

Large brandy glasses
Mixing bowl
Ice cream scoop or strong spoon

Assembly Instructions

Defrost the frozen raspberries and put them in the mixing bowl. Pour the brandy over them and mix gently so that you don't mash up the raspberries. Leave the mixture to macerate as long as possible, overnight in the fridge if possible.

Immediately prior to serving, put a large scoop of the raspberry sherbet into each brandy glass. Divide the mixture equally between the servings, and pour it over the sherbet in each glass.

BAKED DESSERTS

Some desserts, pies for example, need cooking, but don't let that worry you. They are much easier than you think.

Lemon Meringue Pie

The next two desserts use meringue. This requires you to separate the white of the egg from the yolk, as described in Chapter 3.

Parts List

1 frozen uncooked pie shell
3 eggs
1 15 oz (425 gm) can of lemon pie filling
1/3 cup (80 mL) of sugar

Tools Required

Egg separator or clean hands
Electric mixer
Bowl
Can opener
Table spoon

Assembly Instructions

Turn on the oven to 400°F, put the shelf in the middle. Take the frozen pie shell out of its package and allow to thaw in the aluminum foil dish. When the oven is up to temperature and the pie shell is thawed, put it in the oven for 10 minutes. Take it out when the shell is golden brown, and allow it to cool without removing it from the pie plate. Turn off the oven.

Separate the white from the yolks of the three eggs. Do each egg separately in case you break the yolk. (Put the yolk in the refrigerator to use for scrambled eggs for tomorrow's breakfast.) Put the white into a bowl for beating. Add the sugar, and beat using the electric mixer. Meringue is beaten correctly when it is stiff enough to form peaks when the beater is pulled out. Don't beat it beyond that. If the peaks fall down it is not yet ready, but it is possible to beat it too much and the liquid will separate out. It is then scrap.

Open the can of lemon pie filling and fill the pie shell. Turn the BROILER on to 500°F and move the shelf to the top of the oven for broiling. Spoon the meringue onto the top of the filling so that the entire surface of the filling is covered with deep meringue. Place the pie under the broiler and watch it carefully until the top of the pie has turned golden brown. This will happen quite quickly.

Remove from the oven. The pie is ready to serve when cool. Cut into slices when you are serving it.

Baked Alaska

(Serves 4 to 6.) This is another simple but spectacular dessert to serve. People are always impressed when you cook ice cream without melting it. The secret of the dessert is to cover the ice cream completely with meringue to insulate it from the heat. A very high heat is used to bake the outside of the meringue before the heat can reach the ice cream.

Parts List

> 1 small block of hard frozen ice cream
> 1 piece of sponge cake about 1" (25 mm) thick
> 4 eggs
> 1 cup (250 mL) of sugar
> Glace cherries

Tools Required

> Electric beater
> Sharp knife
> Small wooden cutting board, about 1/2" thick
> Aluminum foil
> Mixing bowl
> Egg separator or clean hand

Assembly Instructions

Turn the oven on to 500°F and place the shelf so that the Baked Alaska will fit in the middle.

Cover the wooden cutting board with the aluminum foil. This will be the serving tray. Cut the sponge cake to the same size as the plan cross section of the block of ice cream, and lay it in the middle of the cutting board.

Separate the white from the yolk of the eggs (see the lemon meringue pie recipe), put it in the mixing bowl, add the sugar and beat until it is stiff and firm. Take the ice cream out of the freezer, unwrap it and place it on the sponge cake. Now take the meringue and cover all of the ice cream and sides of the cake liberally with it. This is important because the meringue insulates the ice cream from the heat. Decorate the meringue with glace cherries. Place it in the hot oven carefully. Bake for five minutes until the meringue turns brown on the outside.

Remove and serve immediately at the table. Cut into slices as for a cake.

Brownies

Brownies are a very simple baked dessert which can be served with many modifications. They are very easily made from a bought mix, although some extra ingredients such as eggs, milk and chopped nuts are usually required. They are baked as a single mix in a shallow cake pan and are decorated in the pan before being cut into squares for serving.

Parts List

> 1 package of brownie mix
> Extra ingredients as called for on the package
> Icing sugar

Tools Required

> 8" (200 mm) square baking pan for approximately
>   300 grams of mix
> Tablespoon
> Mixing bowl

Assembly Instructions

Turn on the oven to the required temperature which is usually 350°F. Put the shelf in the centre of the oven. To stop the baked mix from sticking to the pan, put a bit of butter or shortening in the pan and use a piece of waxed paper to spread a thin coating over the entire inside of the pan. The paper taken off a block of butter is ideal for this.

Put the brownie mix into the mixing bowl and add the extra ingredients as specified. Mix as for cement. When the mixing is complete, use the spoon to transfer the mix from the bowl to the baking pan and spread it fairly evenly, but don't be too particular as the oven heat will finish the job for you. Put the pan in the oven when the oven is hot, and cook for the specified time, typically 25 to 30 minutes.

Remove the pan from the oven using oven mitts, turn the oven off and leave the brownies to cool. When they are cool, they can be decorated. A very simple decoration is to use a spoon to sprinkle icing sugar over the top; the white powder contrasts well with the chocolate brownie.

Serving. Cut up the cake into equal sized squares. Usually the hard crust around the side is discarded or given to the people in the family who 'want a taste.' Brownies can be served as little cakes, or they are very good served with ice cream. Put the brownie on a plate and place a scoop of ice cream on top. Pour chocolate sauce over the top. Kids love it.

Rice Crispie Squares

Don't overlook the recipes on the side of packages when considering what to cook. Many of these are designed to be simple and to use that product, so you already have half the ingredients. The following recipe was recommended to me by my wife's Uncle Leonard who took it off a package of Kellogg's Rice Crispies.

Parts List

> 1/4 cup (60mL) of butter
> 5 cups (1.25 L) of miniature marshmallows
> 1/2 teaspoon (3 mL) of vanilla
> 6 cups (1.5 L) of Kellogg's Rice Crispies

Tools Required

> 13 x 9" (330 x 230 mm) baking pan
> Sharp knife
> Mixing bowl
> Saucepan large enough to hold ingredients
> Tablespoon

Assembly Instructions

Put the butter in the saucepan, put the pan on the stove, and turn the heat to medium. Melt the butter. When the butter is melted, turn the heat down and add the marshmallows. Stir until they have melted, then take the pan off the stove, turn off the stove, and then stir in the vanilla. While the mixture is still warm, stir in the Rice Crispies until they are thoroughly coated with the marshmallows. Spoon the mixture into the baking pan and trowel it flat with the back of the spoon; allow to cool. When it is cool, cut into squares.

TWO WHIPPED CREAM DESSERTS

As stated before, whipped cream can turn the ordinary dessert into an exotic masterpiece. These two examples are quite easy to make but look quite difficult.

Strawberry Wonder

(Serves 8.) It's made with strawberries and whipped cream and everybody wonders how you made it. You need to be able to buy an angel food cake from the store. That is a large, white, donut shaped cake which looks like styrofoam.

Parts List

> 1 angel food cake
> 1 packet of frozen strawberries
> 1 large container (500 mL) carton of whipping cream
> 2 teaspoons (10 mL) of sugar

Tools Required

> Electric mixer
> Mixing bowl
> Sharp knife
> Tablespoon
> Spatula

Assembly Instructions

Cut the angel food cake in the radial plane so that you have two thin donuts instead of one thick one. It is easier to do this by freezing the cake first and then cutting it with a bread saw. Thaw the frozen strawberries.

Pour the whipping cream into the mixing bowl and add the sugar. Beat with the electric mixer until the liquid becomes stiff. When it is ready the cream will form peaks when the beater is removed. Be careful not to beat longer than this point because the cream will separate into butter and butter milk. (At least you can always spread the butter on some bread.)

When the cream is whipped, open the packet of strawberries. Combine the contents with the whipped cream by folding the cream over the strawberries very carefully. Do not stir or destroy the texture of the whipped cream. Place one half of the angel food cake on a plate with the cut side up. Using the same technique as you would to butter bricks with mortar to make a brick wall, use the palette knife as a trowel and spread some of the cream mixture liberally onto the cut side of the cake. When it is about 1/2" thick, place the cut side of the other piece on top to form a sandwich.

Now cover the entire cake with the strawberry and cream mixture so that none of the cake shows; include the sides in the hole. The entire cake can be decorated with fresh strawberries when they are in season.

Keep in the fridge and serve the same day.

English Trifle

(Serves 12.) This easy dish always looks impressive. It is a good dessert to take to a potluck since it is easy to carry and serves a lot of people (or a few fat ones).

Parts List

1 package of individual swiss rolls
1 package of strawberry jelly
2 15 oz (425 gm) tins of Devon custard (If you prefer you can make the equivalent quantity of Bird's custard. Follow the instructions on the tin.)
1 small carton (250 mL) of whipping cream
1 banana
1/2 cup (125 mL) of sherry
1/2 bottle (22 mL) of rum flavouring
1 packet of sprinkles
1 packet (425 gm) of frozen strawberries
1 teaspoonful (5 mL) of sugar

Tools Required

1 large deep serving bowl
Electric mixer
Kettle
Two mixing bowls
Tablespoon
Spatula
Sharp knife

Assembly Instructions

Defrost the strawberries. Slice the swiss rolls into eighths and place them flat in the bottom of the serving bowl. Sprinkle the sherry and rum flavouring over the top. Allow the liquid to soak into the cake for a few minutes, then pour the strawberries over the top. Make up the jelly following the instructions on the package, but using half the specified quantity of water. When mixed, pour this into the bowl with the other ingredients, and then put the bowl in the fridge for the jelly to set. Leave it for a couple of hours.

If you are using Bird's custard, make it up now and allow it to cool. When the jelly is set, pour the custard into the bowl, and trowel it even with the back of the spoon. Peel and slice the banana in the transverse plane into round slices, and place the slices on the custard. It does not matter if they sink into the custard. Put the whipping cream into the other mixing bowl and add the sugar. Whip the cream using the mixer until it is firm, then trowel the cream over the surface of the custard so that the entire top surface is whipping cream. When ready to serve at the table, sprinkle the top with multicolored sprinkles.

THE BIRTHDAY PARTY

The phone rings and it's your daughter.

"Dad, I need to ask you a favour; are you busy."

Right away you should be suspicious; however, unsuspecting you press on.

"No"

"You remember it's Junior's birthday tomorrow?"

"Yes." Actually you have clean forgotten about it. Who said you had to change your ways because you are a househusband.

"Well, I've just heard that I have to work late tomorrow. Marc's out of town and I've invited a whole bunch of kids over for the party at 3:30. Can you help me out and keep an eye on them?"

"Well, I might be able to," but before you can think up a suitable excuse you hear:

"Gee, Dad that's great, I knew I could rely on you. Everything is ready so don't worry."

At this point you start to worry; some little bell is ringing.

"What do you mean everything is ready?" you ask.

"I've cleaned the furniture, changed the beds, put the good china away, washed Junior's party clothes; everything is done."

"What about the food?"

"Oh. I haven't had time to do that, but I know you are home all day and I thought you wouldn't mind doing that to help out. Sorry the boss has just come in and I have to go. Thanks again, Dad. Bye"

And that's it.

It may not be exactly like that; there are many scenarios, but the result is the same. You've inherited a birthday party. What to do?

The first and most important thing to do is arrange for the birthday cake. You must have a cake with candles on even if you cook it yourself in the microwave. However, I suggest you get the cake from the local bakery; they do a good job of icing and they can personalise it with the name in five minutes. The cake itself doesn't matter but it must have the correct number of candles on it, and you MUST spell the name right.

"Did you have a good time at your party dear? Sorry mummy couldn't make it sooner."

"No! My name was spelt wrong on the cake and there were only five candles and I'm six!!"

There is nothing difficult about preparing the food for a birthday party. Junior does not want a sumptuous feast, the secret is to serve it up differently so that it looks like a birthday party. The following recipes give ideas on how to change simple things into something different.

The ubiquitous hot dog is a great favourite with the junior set and it is very easy to dress it up to look like something else. These two suggestions are created using a simple piece of triangular paper or a folded napkin, and a toothpick or bamboo skewer.

Jet Dog

Dress up the hot dog to look like a jet plane as shown in Figure 9. Cut two pieces of paper into triangles. Make the hot dog in the usual way, then put a 6" bamboo skewer through the hot dog and bun, or use two toothpicks to hold the 'wings' on as shown in the diagram.

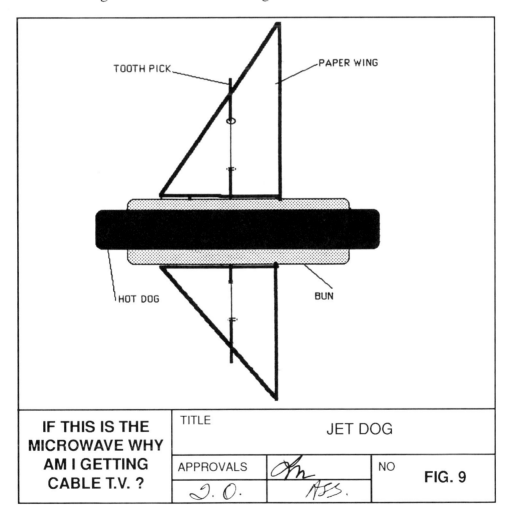

IF THIS IS THE MICROWAVE WHY AM I GETTING CABLE T.V. ?	TITLE	JET DOG	
	APPROVALS		NO
	J. O.		FIG. 9

Junk Dog

Since hot dogs are usually considered junk food, I couldn't think of a better description for the boat than a 'junk dog.' Use the same shape for the sails as for the jet wings, but put them on top of the dog instead of on the side, as shown in Figure 10. For the 'junk' just use tooth picks; the skewers would be too long.

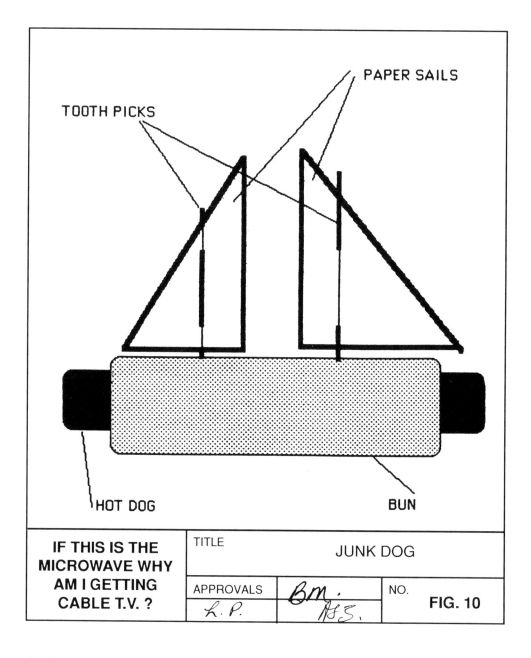

IF THIS IS THE MICROWAVE WHY AM I GETTING CABLE T.V. ?	TITLE	JUNK DOG		
	APPROVALS	*Bm.*	NO.	FIG. 10
	L. P.	*AJS.*		

Ice cream is another favourite with the kids; these ideas are very simple to use and turn a regular dish of ice cream into something special. Vanilla ice cream is usually best for these since the colours show up better.

Ice Cream Clowns

Very easy to do as you can see in Figure 11. Take a regular ice cream cone and fill it with a generous scoop of ice cream. Now turn the cone upside down onto a plate and set the cone at an angle. Put on eyes, a nose, and if there is room add a mouth and ears. If you use coloured smarties it will look quite festive.

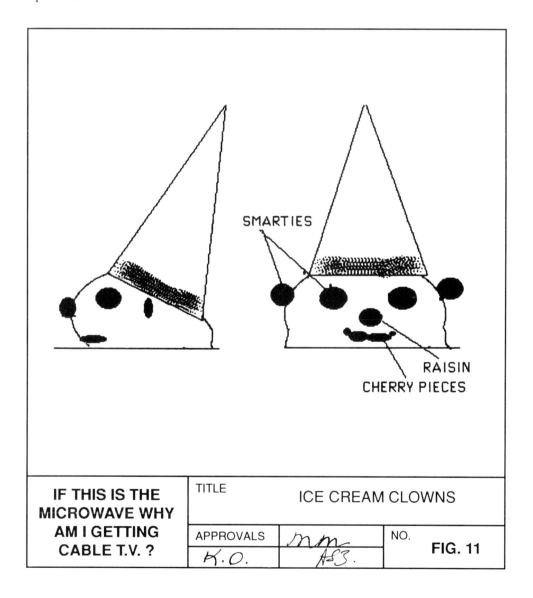

IF THIS IS THE MICROWAVE WHY AM I GETTING CABLE T.V. ?	TITLE	ICE CREAM CLOWNS	
	APPROVALS	*mm*	NO.
	K.O.	*ASS.*	**FIG. 11**

SMARTIES

RAISIN
CHERRY PIECES

Mice Cream

Another very simple idea is shown in Figure 12. This time put the ice cream directly into the serving dish. Use raisins for the eyes and nostrils and then add two chocolate wafers to make the large mouse ears. Push the wafers into the ice cream to get them to hold. Finally get some thin licorice and make the whiskers.

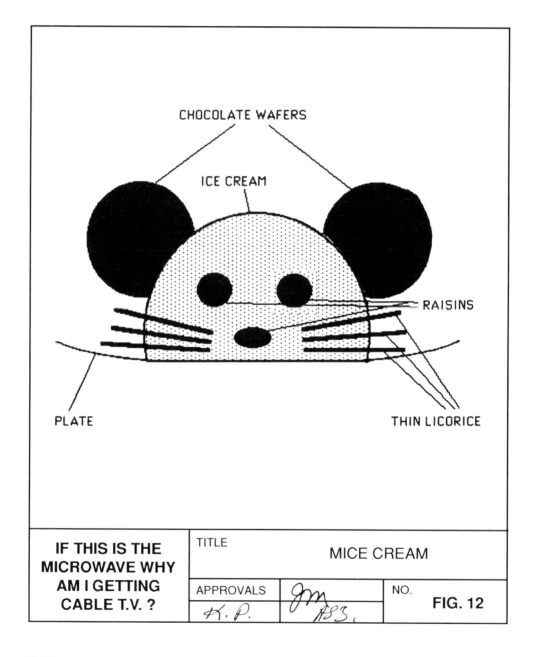

IF THIS IS THE MICROWAVE WHY AM I GETTING CABLE T.V. ?	TITLE	MICE CREAM		
	APPROVALS	*m*	NO.	FIG. 12
	K. P.	*ABS.*		

9. THE FAT
(FAMILY ACCEPTANCE TEST)
How to Manage Turkeys

Taking stock of all the things that you have learnt in this book, you have learnt how to:

A) Prepare food by:

> • Opening packages
> • Cutting (slicing, peeling, shredding, etc.)
> • Mixing

B) Cook food by:

> • Boiling (water, soup, vegetables, etc.)
> • Frying
> • Slow cooking
> • Microwaving
> • Broiling
> • Baking
> • Toasting

Using these techniques you have prepared Experimental Prototypes and have graduated through Development Models to Mature Products. You have also learned how to utilize Field Support, and you can manage Software problems. In the process you may well have ruined enough food to feed the Third World, but eventually you have persevered and you now believe that you can create CANS (remember? Cook A Nice Supper). Good! You can now produce CANS and have it inspected.

The inspection is known as the FAT, or Family Acceptance Test. As with all final inspections, everybody and his brother will be hanging around to watch and criticize, so why not invite all the relatives over for the CANS inspection. They will come anyway.

HOW TO MANAGE TURKEYS

At the beginning of this handbook you were promised instructions on dealing with turkeys and you should now have reached the stage where you can follow the directions. For the FAT you will assume the responsibility of Househusband In Charge of the Kitchen (HICK), and you will be required to provide a sample of CANS to the specification provided. At each stage of the manufacture you will present the result for inspection and evaluation and the procedure will continue until all subassemblies of CANS have been completed. All disputes will be referred to the Head of the Household (HOH) for resolution (and I'm not getting into that one). The decision of the HOH shall be final and binding on all parties.

CANS Specification

Turkey Dinner

Soup

Swamp Water Soup

Entrée

Roast Boss Turkey with Employee Stuffing

and

Ministry Sauce

Carrots a la Finance

Sprouts Personnel

Executive Mashed Potatoes

Dessert

Golden Handshake Trifle

Hard Grind Coffee

Inspection Procedure

General Product Description

The product CANS described in this specification is for a Turkey Dinner (TD) to be prepared, without assistance, by the HICK. The TD will be prepared following GMP (Good Meal Preparation) procedures and must be edible when finished. The final decision on the edibility of the TD shall be made by the HOH. Other interested parties in the FDA (Family Dining Area) may comment, but may not take part in the final decision. However, they are invited to submit written criticism of the product or process. Such criticism will be processed and suitable actions will be taken.

Documentation

The following document of the exact issue shown forms a part of this specification to the extent specified herein. In the event of conflict between the document referenced herein and the contents of this specification, the contents of this specification shall be considered a superceding requirement.

MIL LTR 1111   "Make it Look Like The Recipe For Once"

Schedule

The schedule for the production of the individual portions of CANS is critical to ensure that the TD does not deteriorate through delay. The inspection department will be authorised to accept items which have been subjected to unavoidable delays.

Requirements

The TD shall be prepared in the sequence shown, i.e. soup, entrée, and dessert, and it is essential that the items be presented in that order. Where subassemblies form part of the main assembly item, as for example in the entrée, all these sub assemblies must be presented for inspection at the same time as the main assembly.

    The inspectors are not required or expected to be present during the preparation of the TD by the HICK, but are expected to be present for the final inspection. If any inspector delays the inspection process for any reason whether they be drunk or sober, the HICK shall not be held responsible for quitting 'cold turkey.'

Preparation Procedure

It is essential that long lead items be tackled first to ensure that the main items are presented in the correct order. The following sequence is the preferred approach. Check the sequence carefully and determine the probable program elapsed time 'E.' Allow adequate time for the raw material processing. Determine the required delivery time 'T' and calculate the required start time 'S' from $S = (T - E) - 1.0$

Trifle Pre-preparation

At time 'S' begin the trifle preparation. The HICK should prepare the basic trifle first to allow sufficient time for the fruit and jelly to set. Refer to the recipe for English Trifle. Make up the recipe to the point where the trifle is put in the fridge for a couple of hours. If the HICK elects to make the trifle with Bird's custard, this should be made up at this time and cooled in the fridge also.

Turkey Roasting

It is recommended that the turkey be cooked in aluminum foil because this process is easier and quicker, and it is less likely that the bird will be incinerated.

Parts List

1 12 to 15 lb (6 -7 Kg) recently defrosted turkey
Turkey stuffing:
      3/4 loaf of unsliced bread
      4 medium onions
      1/2 lb (225 gm) mushrooms
      1 cup (250 mL) of diced celery
      1/2 lb (250 gm) butter
      1 cup (250 mL) of cold water
      Poultry seasoning to taste
      Package of Knorr Fine Herb soup mix
Salt
Potatoes
Carrots
Sprouts
1 tin cranberry sauce or jelly
Packet of gravy thickening
1 tin (284 mL) of mushroom soup
Select Wine as required or desired

The quantities of potatoes, carrots, sprouts and wine will depend on the size of the inspection staff present. Allow more for 200 lb inspectors than for 50 lb inspectors. The decision to use frozen or fresh carrots or sprouts shall be the responsibility of the HICK providing adequate supplies of each are available from stores.

Tools Required

> Large roasting pan for the turkey
> (This is very important. It can be very embarrassing to prepare the turkey and find that you have forgotten the roasting pan or that the pan you have is not big enough.)
> 1 roll heavy duty 18" (457 mm) wide aluminum foil
> 4 Small Skewers
> Suitable pans for:
>> custard
>> potatoes
>> sprouts
>> carrots
>> gravy
> Carving knife and carving fork
> Vegetable peeler or sharp knife
> Bread knife
> Trifle bowl
> Serving dishes
> Corkscrew

Assembly Instructions

Turkey Preparation

Examine the turkey carefully. There are two major cavities, the neck cavity and the other end. The other end can be recognized because the end of the legs will be stuffed into it; perhaps this is why some people are referred to as turkeys. Open the flap which covers the neck cavity and remove any paper package which may be in there. Do not discard! Move to the other end and release the end of the legs so the inside of the bird can be accessed. Remove any items which are inside the bird; these will usually consist of another paper package and the neck. Again do not discard; the contents from the neck and body will be used to make gravy stock.

Wash inside both of the cavities with running water, pat dry with a paper towel, and rub the cavity walls with salt.

Stuffing

Stuffing is packed inside the turkey to support the rib cage during cooking. Cut up the loaf of bread into 1" (25 mm) cubes. Peel and slice the onions into small pieces. Wash the mushrooms thoroughly and cut off the brown ends of the stems. Cut the mushrooms into halves. Prepare the celery, and cut it up into 1/4" (5 mm) lengths to get a cupful of pieces.

Put all the ingredients into a large bowl with the bread, and mix them together like you would prepare a dry mix for concrete. Sprinkle poultry seasoning over the mix. Melt the butter in the microwave or use a medium/low heat and melt it in a pan on the stove; pour it over the contents of the bowl. Use two spoons to stir as for a tossed salad. Add a small quantity of water and mush everything together by hand. It should bind together, but not be wet and soggy.

Take the stuffing mix and push liberal quantities into the neck cavity until the cavity is full. Raise the neck flap and close the opening by pinning it to the turkey body with one or two of the small skewers. Now stuff the body cavity. and restore the legs to the original position. Locate the wings and pin them to the side of the bird with skewers.

Turkey Roasting

Unroll 3 or 4 feet of the aluminum foil and place it on the counter top. Some turkeys have a string harness supplied to assist in removing the bird from the roasting pan, this should be put on the turkey now. Place the turkey in the centre of the foil, and wrap the foil around the body so that all the flesh is covered. Place the turkey in the roasting pan.

Turn on the oven and place the rack on a low level so that there is enough room for the turkey. Put the turkey in the oven and turn the temperature to 450°F. Set the timer for the correct cooking time:

> 12 lb. time 3 hrs.
> 15 lb. time 3 1/4 hrs.

Calculate the time when the turkey will be ready.

Gravy Stock Preparation

Open up the packages that were inside the bird; these will contain the heart, and other organs. Put them in a pan with water, put the lid on and bring the water to a boil on the stove. Turn the heat down to low. Boiling them will produce good stock for the gravy. Allow the gravy stock to simmer until it is required, but watch it carefully to see that it doesn't boil dry. If the liquid gets low, add more water.

Vegetable Preparation

When the turkey is safely in the oven and the door is closed, start preparing the vegetables. Peel the potatoes, and put them in a pan covered in water; do not cook at this time. Fresh vegetables should be prepared at this time by the HICK. Peel all fresh vegetables and put them in separate pans, covered with water.

Frozen vegetables should be prepared following the instructions on the packages. If large quantities are to be cooked in the microwave, it is advisable to defrost the vegetables prior to cooking even though the instructions say do not defrost. This is because with large quantities, the defrosting tends to be uneven, and some of the items will be overcooked and some still raw at the end of the cooking time.

The HICK may schedule a quick coffee break at this time.

Scheduling the TD

It is essential that the HICK maintain strict control of the schedule following the coffee break. The following schedule is recommended.

As soon as the coffee break is over, remove the trifle from the fridge and add the custard and the banana. Whip the cream and add it to the top of the bowl, but do not add the sprinkles. Put the trifle back in the fridge.

Prepare the coffee machine for coffee for the inspection team.

Open the tin of cranberry sauce and put it in a sauce dish.

Half an hour prior to the serving time 'T' i.e. at ('T' - 0.5) remove the turkey from the oven so that it can cool. This will make the bird easier to carve. Remove the top of the aluminum foil, and check that the meat is beginning to pull back from the end of the legs. This indicates that the bird is cooked; leave covered in the foil on the counter top. If the bird is not yet cooked, report that everything is on schedule and put the bird back in the oven for a further half hour. (Remember, never report that you are falling behind schedule.) When the bird is ready to remove from the oven, turn the heat down to 200°F.

Put the potatoes on the stove, turn the heat to high and bring them to the boil; add salt as required. If fresh carrots are being used for the FAT, put them on to boil also at this time. When boiling, turn the heat down and note the time.

Final Assembly

Swamp Water Soup

Swamp Water Soup is made from a package of dried herb soup mix. When cooked the green herbs float on the top and my family insists that it resembles swamp water, but it's very good tasting swamp water. It can be cooked while the vegetables are cooking.

Start the soup, following the instructions on the package, and stir frequently.

Cooking Vegetables

After ten minutes put the sprouts on to boil. Check that the gravy stock has not boiled dry.

If frozen vegetables are being used start cooking them at ('T'- 0.25). As soon as the carrots are cooked, transfer them to the serving bowl, sprinkle brown sugar over the top and put a piece of butter or margarine on them. Put a cover on the dish and put them in the oven to keep warm. The sprouts should also be done by this time, transfer them to a covered serving dish, put a piece of butter on them, and put them in the oven. Finally mash the potatoes with some butter and 1/2 cup (125 mL) of sour cream, and put them in the oven.

Gravy

Remove the meat from the gravy stock and discard it. Open the can of mushroom soup, add it to the stock and use a fork or a whisk to mix it thoroughly. If necessary put in some gravy thickening following the instructions on the package, and thicken the gravy. Pour the gravy into a serving jug and put it in the oven.

Serving

Peel back the aluminum foil from the turkey, and carve the required amount of meat off the bird. Put the meat on a platter and cover it with some aluminum foil to prevent it from drying out. Put it in the oven.

Serve the soup in individual bowls. Turn off the stove and oven.

As soon as the soup is finished, remove the meat and vegetables from the oven and transfer them to the table. Pass the dishes round for the inspectors to serve themselves, return to the kitchen and fetch the gravy, the cranberry sauce and the wine.

Turn on the coffee machine.

When the entrée is finished, put the sprinkles on the trifle and serve it with the coffee. The inspection is complete.

That Was It

Candles Lit

Guests Were Fine

And The Wine

All Was Good

With The Food

What Is Best

You Passed The Test

You Can Cook

End Of Book !!

APPENDECTOMY
Removing the Myth From Metric

You are now ready to use real recipe books since you now know what they are trying to say. There is, however, one last thing to confront: the confusing system of weights and measures which is used in the books and which frequently defies all rational. Take for example the term 'a cup of.' Who defines the size of the cup? Are we looking for Lord Stanley's version, or are we looking for a size 36C? Are we supposed to 'cup' our hands and scoop out the required quantity? After considerable research, much of it spent while in my cups, I have put together some information to help you translate such terms.

There are four basic measurement systems used in cooking, the American system, the British system, the European (metric) system, and the GM (Grandmother) system. The GM system has units of 'Smidgens,' 'Slurps,' 'Dollops,' 'About That Much' and 'Ahelluvalotof.' I have been unable to rationalize these units with the other three systems and the GM system is only mentioned here because you are sure to meet it sometime. Although the metric system is now used almost universally throughout the world, many cookbooks have been written using either the American or British systems. Prior to the introduction of the metric system into Canada, the British Imperial measure was frequently used as indicated in the table. The following table describes the basic units; abbreviations are as follows:

Millimetres	=	mm	Inches	=	in
Centimetres	=	cm	Feet	=	ft
Meters	=	m	Ounces	=	oz
Kilometres	=	Km	Pounds	=	lb
Grams	=	gm	Gallons	=	gals
Kilograms	=	Kg			
Millilitres	=	mL			
Litres	=	l			

Remember for cooking, machine shop precision is not required and the conversions are rounded off. For example 1 cm = 0.393701 in., but this has been rounded to 0.4 in.

BASIC UNITS

METRIC	AMERICAN	CANADIAN (BRITISH)
1 cm	0.4 in	0.4 in
10 mm	0.4 in	0.4 in
100 gm	3.5 oz	3.5 oz
200 gm	7.0 oz	7.0 oz
225 gm	0.5 lb	0.5 lb

. . . continued on page 158

METRIC	AMERICAN	CANADIAN
450 gm	1 lb	1 lb
1000 gm	2.2 lb	2.2 lb
(1 kilogram)		
30 mL	1 oz (1.014)	1 oz (1.05)
120 mL	4 oz	4 oz
240 mL	8 oz	8.5 oz
450 mL	15 oz	16 oz
738.7 mL	25 oz	26 oz
1 litre	1 quart approx.	35 oz
2 litres	2 quarts approx	70 oz
3.8 litres	1 gal	133 oz
4.5 litres	1.2 gal	1 gal

Velocity of Light = 299,792.5 Km per second
= 186,000 miles per second (approximately).

So what's that got to do with cooking? Well it's the speed that the microwaves and infra-red heat travel around in your ovens. It's a bit of useless information now, but it may prove useful in the future. In your next interview when you are asked to describe yourself, just say "Well I do my cooking at 186,000 miles per second" and see what sort of impression you can create. (Remember to use kilometres if it's a government interview.)

BASIC MEASUREMENTS

UNIT	METRIC	BRITISH
1 cup (liquid)	250 mL	8 oz
1 cup	16 tablespoons	16 tablespoons
5 cups	1200 mL	40 oz, 1 quart
2 tablespoons	30 mL	1 oz
1 tablespoon	3 teaspoons, 15 mL	3 teaspoons
1 teaspoon	5 mL	1/6 oz
1 dessertspoon	2 teaspoons, 10 mL	2 teaspoons
1 dash	0.3 teaspoon	1/3 teaspoon
1 pinch	0.25 teaspoon	1/4 teaspoon
1 pony	30 mL	1 oz

Using these relationships and a bit of common sense it is possible to measure out most quantities required. You can now follow the recipe, and if it calls for a cup of rice, you now know what they mean. If the recipe specifies a unit which you cannot convert, there is usually a way to overcome the difficulty. If it specifies metric units and your package is in metric, then measure out the required fraction of the package; you don't have to be too precise. The situation gets to be more challenging if the recipe calls for pounds and your package is in grams. Calculate the weight required in grams using 450 grams to 1 pound, and again use proportion to measure.

INVENTORY

TOOL CRIB

WORKSHOP PRACTICE
Hand Tools 16-18
Power Tools 18
Safety First 15

TERMINOLOGY

Baking 22, 33, 34
Boiling 23, 33, 34
....................................43, 46
Broiling 33, 34
Brown 22
Calories 27
Eggs Breaking 30
Eggs Separating 30-31
Eggs White 30-31
Eggs Yolk 30-31
Frying 33-34, 47
Liquid Flavourings 36-37
Macerate 37
Marinate 37
Microwaves 33, 34, 51
Mixing 33
MRP 11, 25-27
Mumbo Jumbo 22-24
Nutrition 27-28
Peeling 29,32
Roasting 33, 34, 96-97
Seasonings 35-36, 67
Shredding 32
Simmering 33, 34
Slicing 33
Slow Cooking 33, 35
Tearing 32
Toasting 33, 34
Trimming 32
Understanding recipes 21

COMPONENTS

PROTOTYPES

Boiled Egg 46
Coffee 42
Grapefruit 40-41
Hot Soup 45, 62, 103
Microwave Cake 51
Muffins 48-50
Omelette 7
Quick Chili 53
Tea 43
The Super Bowl 52-53
Toast 44, 55, 56, 57, 58, 59, 60

ACCESSORIES

SAUCES

Cheese Sauce 102
White Sauce 101

SUB ASSEMBLIES

DEVELOPMENT MODELS

Canadian Rarebit 60-61
Cowboy beans on Toast 56
Sardines on Toast 58
Scrambled Eggs on Toast 57
Soup and Grilled Cheese Sandwich 62
Welsh Rarebit 59

COMPLETE ASSEMBLIES

AFTERBURNERS

Bubble and Squeak 108
Hot Meat Sandwich 108
Reheating 108

CASSEROLES

Househusband Casserole 73
Shepherds Pie 74
Yellow Green Bean Surprise 75

CURRIES

Curried Turkey 84-85
Curry in a Bag 86-87

FISH

Bajun Salmon Poached in Wine 100
Sole and Parsley Sauce 99

MEAT

Dad's Beef Pot Roast 94-95
Ginger Beef and Brocoli 92-93
Honey Chicken 89
Horse Meat Deluxe 91
Mixed Grill 90
Oven Roasting 96
Pork Chops and Mushroom Sauce 88
Roast Beef and
        Yorkshire Pudding 96-98
Roast Turkey 147-154
Turkey 84, 96, 103, 108, 147-154

PASTA

Lasagna 79-80
Linguini and Clam Sauce 78
Spaghetti 76-77

PIES

Cheese and Ham Pie 81-82
Rice Cheese and Tomato 83

SALADS

Caesar 105
Creamy Potato 106-107
Simple 103-104

STEWS

Dad's Famous Farmhouse 67-68
Hungarian Goulash 71-72
Vegetable 69-70

SOFTWARE PROGRAMS

BAKED DESERTS

Baked Alaska 135
Brownies 136
Lemon Meringue Pie 134
Rice Crispie Squares 137

BIRTHDAY PARTY

Ice Cream Clowns 145
Jet Dog 143
Junk Dog 144
Mice Cream 146

ICE CREAM

Parfait 132
Raspberry Delight 133
Sundaes 131-132

WHIPPED CREAM

English Trifle 140-141
Strawberry Wonder 138-139

FIELD SPARES

FROZEN VEGETABLES

Convetional Cooking 110
Microwave Cooking 111

GREEN VEGETABLES

Beans French 112
Beans Runner 112
Broccoli 92, 101, 112, 115, 125
Brussels Sprouts 33, 112, 113
Cabbage 32, 103, 112
Cauliflower 101, 112, 114, 125
Lettuce 32, 103, 105, 112
Peas 112

ONIONS

Garlic 26, 123, 124
Leeks 123, 124
Regular 36, 123,
Spring 123

RICE
Boiled 83, 128
Microwave 128

ROOT VEGETABLES
Carrots 32, 49, 119
Parsnips 32, 120
Potatoes Boiled 32, 116-117
Potatoes Mashed 32, 117-118
Potato Salad 106
Rutabaga 32, 120

SALADS, RAW
Apples 125, 126
Broccoli Head 125
Carrots 125, 126
Cauliflower 125
Cucumber 125, 126
Green Peppers 125, 126
Mushrooms 125, 126
Tomato 125, 126
Zucchini 125, 126

SQUASH
Acorn Squash 121-122
Zucchini 122

VALIDATION PROTOCOLS

FAMILY ACCEPTANCE TEST (FAT)
CANS Specification 148
Documentation 149
Inspection Procedure 149
Product Description 149
Requirements 149
Schedule 149-154
Turkey Preparation 151
Turkey Roasting 150, 152
How to Serve a Turkey 154

If you wish to order additional copies of

If this is the microwave, why am I getting cable t.v. ?

send cheque or money order for $15.95 CAN + 2.00 per book for shipping + 7 % G.S.T. (TOTAL 19.21) to:

Creative Bound Inc.
P.O. Box 424,
151 Tansley Road,
Carp Ontario K0A 1L0

* for trade discounts, U.S., Overseas or VISA orders, call (613) 831-3641